Discovering Color behind the Keys

The Essence of the Russian School of Piano-Playing

Rada Bukhman

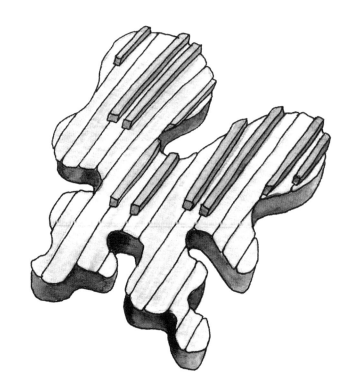

Illustrations: Anna Vetrova

Photography and Digital Images Processing: Alexander Bukhman

Music Notation and Layout Editing: Anna Yuferova

Text Editing: Michael Bukhman, Julie Sutherland

ISBN: 978-0-9918225-0-8

Acknowledgements

My book would not be complete without contributions of a few talented contemporary composers, the families of the outstanding composers of the twentieth century who kindly granted permission to publish many of the original works, and without help of my dear friends and family.

I would like to express my deep gratitude to Russian composers Mikhail Zhuravlev, Efrem Podgaits, Mikhail Shukh, and Valery Saparov. Their works are well known and popular in Russia and Europe, and it is my privilege to bring them to the attention of the musical community of North America.

I am honored to include in this book the works of composer Alexander Lokshin, who studied with Nikolay Myaskovsky and whom Dmitri Shostakovich called a genius. The tragic life of Alexander Lokshin made his piano music almost unknown to Western audiences. I am grateful to A. Lokshin - the composer's son - who gave me permission to publish his father's music.

The fate of music by another distinguished Russian Composer, Georgy Sviridov, was more favorable, and his works are well known in the West. However, this is the first book to present his piano pieces written for children to the Canadian and American public. I would like to thank Professor Alexander Belonenko - the nephew of the composer - for his permission to include in this book pieces from Sviridov's *Children's Album*.

The music of the famous educator and composer of music for children, Samuel Maykapar, is loved around the world. My deep appreciation goes to his grandson, Professor Alexander Maikapar, for his approval to publish pieces of his renowned grandfather in this book.

I am also grateful to Mrs. Nadezhda Volkova for her permission to publish the works for children by the composer, V. Volkov, who was her father.

Additionally, this book would certainly not be the same without the illustrations of the extremely talented artist, Anna Vetrova.

Many thanks also go to Anna Yuferova for her highly professional help in printing musical scores and preparing the book for publication.

As well, I greatly appreciate the editing assistance provided by Michael Bukhman and Julie Sutherland.

I am also very grateful to my friends and colleagues from Russia, Olga Repina and Konstantin Yudin, for their help and encouragement along the way.

Finally, I am profoundly grateful to my husband, Alexander, who provided professional assistance with photography and the post-processing of digital images. Most importantly, he gave me inspiration, encouragement, and constant help. Without these, this project would not have been possible.

To my parents Gennady and Mary Kharibi

Table of Contents

Preface 11

Developing Initial Musical Skills 13

On the Nature and Development of a Musical Ear 13

On Rhythm 14

Preparatory Stages 15

Sight-Reading 16

The Means of Expression in Performance 17

Sound Production 17

Dynamics 18

The Art of Phrasing 20

Sustain Pedal 22

Developing Fundamentals of Piano Technique 23

The Nature of Pianistic Movements 23

Tension and Relaxation 24

Position at the Piano 25

Establishing Contact with Keyboard 25

Hand Position 25

Touching the Keyboard 26

First Steps 28

Exercises and Pieces for the Third Finger 29

Paraphrases 33

Alexander Borodin, Polka 33

Nikolay Rimsky-Korsakov, Minuet 34

Exercises and Pieces Using the Second and Fourth Fingers 35

Wolfgang Amadeus Mozart, Theme from Variations 36

The Thumb 38

The Fifth Finger 40

Five fingers Exercises and Pieces 41

Samuel Maykapar, Two easy pieces for piano 4 hands (From "First Steps") 43

Anton Arensky, The Crane (Composition for Piano Four Hands) 47

Michael Shukh, Orange Choo-choo Train 48

Ludwig Shitte, Study No.1 49

Ludwig Shitte, Study No.2 50

Development of Motor Skills 51

Exercises and Pieces for the Development of Motor Skills 53

Vjacheslav Volkov, Joke 57

Daniel Gottlob Turk, Spring Song 57

Leopold Mozart, From Notebook, Burlesque 58

Michael Shukh, Buzzing Bee 58

Cornelius Gurlitt, Little Dance 59

Ludwig Shitte, Study 59

Cornelius Gurlitt, Game for Two C. Gurlitt 60

Cornelius Gurlitt, Melody 61

Daniel Gottlob Turk, Ballett 61

Daniel Gottlob Turk, Happy Hours 62

Cezar Cui, Russian Dance (Composition for Piano Four Hands) 63

Anton Arensky, The Cuckoo (Composition for Piano Four Hands) 65

Playing Legato 69

Vjacheslav Volkov, Echo 72

Michael Shukh, Lullaby 72

Cornelius Gurlitt, Cheerful Hour 73

Vjacheslav Volkov, Meditation 74

Efrem Podgaits, In a Happy Mood 75

Efrem Podgaits, Sad Song 76

Vjacheslav Volkov, Snowdrop 76

Mikhail Glinka, The Lark 78

Samuel Maykapar, Piece in C Major (Composition for Piano Four Hands. From "First Steps") 80

Cezar Cui, Piece in D Minor (Composition for Piano Four Hands. From "Ten Five-Finger Pieces") 82

Scales, Chords and Arpeggios 85

Scales 85

Broken Chords 87

Solid Chords 88

Arpeggios 88

Dance Voyage 89

Anonymous (From the Notebook of Anna Magdalena Bach), Minuet 90

Wolfgang Amadeus Mozart, Minuet 91

Cornelius Gurlitt, Gavotte 93

Carl Reinecke, Gavotte 94

Wolfgang Amadeus Mozart, Polonaise From "Viennese Sonatina" K439b No.5 98

Cornelius Gurlitt, Mazurka 101

Samuel Maykapar, Mazurka 102

Franz Schubert, Lendler (Composition for Piano Four Hands, arr. By F. List) 105

Victor Kosenko, Waltz 107

Accompaniments in Dances – Waltz, Polka 108

Victor Kosenko, Polka 110

Philipp Emanuel Bach, March (From the Notebook of Anna Magdalena Bach) 114

Children's Albums 116

Robert Schumann, Album for the Young, op. 68 117

Melody 118

Soldier's March 119

Folk Song 120

Happy Farmer 122

Sicilian Dance 123

First Loss 125

Pyotr Ilyich Tchaikovsky Children's Album, op.39 126

March of the Wooden Soldiers 127

Sick Doll 129

Waltz 130

Mazurka 133

Italian Song 135

Old French Song 137

Neapolitan Song 138

Sweet Dream 140

Samuel Maykapar, Biriulki, op.28 142

In the Garden 143

Waltz 144

Exciting Moment 146

Polka 148

Fleeting Apparition 150

Little Commander 151

Fairy Tale 153

Georgy Sviridov, Children's Album 154

Fairy Lullaby 155

Jumping Rope 156

Gentle Request 157

Stubborn Kid 158

Musical Moment 160

Theodor Kullak, Scenes from Childhood op.62 165

Once Upon a Time there Was a Princess 165

Little Cradle Song 167

Sunday Morning 169

On the Playground 171

Alexander Lokshin, Three Pieces for Children 173

Dance 173

Waltz 175

Autumn Rain 177

Mikhail Zhuravlev, Inventions 180

Merry-Go-Round 180

Swing 182

Hide and Seek 184

Sonatinas/Variations/Bagatelle 185

Daniel Gottlieb Steibelt, Sonatina in C Major 185

Carl Maria von Weber, Sonatina for Piano 4 hands Op.3 No.1 ... 189

Samuel Maykapar, Variations on the Russian Theme Op.8 No.14 ... 197

Ludwig van Beethoven, Lustig –Traurig WoO 54 202

Jazz for Barbie 204

Valery Saparov, Waltz for Barbie 205

Valery Saparov, Blues for Barbie 206

Valery Saparov, We Play Jazz, Three Easy Pieces for Piano Four Hands ... 208

With a Smile 208

First Waltz 209

Roly-Poly Doll 211

Preface

Teaching music to children is both interesting and incredibly difficult. At times it feels as though performing an entire solo recital would be easier than teaching the smallest sense of musicality to a young student. The feeling is true even when working with the simplest of little pieces. It is harder to teach than to learn, but by teaching you inevitably learn yourself. Nothing allowed me to advance my own understanding of music and the particularities of piano-playing more than pedagogy.

It has been a wish of mine to compile the professional methods that I encountered through my involvement with the Russian School of piano-playing as well as to share my own teaching experience in a book that would be interesting and useful to teachers, parents, and of course, students.
A book cannot replace a teacher, but it can provide readers with an essence for a pedagogical approach. I trust that my essays on music and pianism will help parents delve deeper into the world in which their child is immersed during a piano lesson. Much of the advice will also be helpful to musicians that are just beginning their teaching careers, as well as to experienced teachers, who will hopefully find some new ideas in my book.

Heinrich Neuhaus is an internationally distinguished musician and pedagogue whose book, *The Art of Piano-Playing*, has been, for many decades, widely regarded as the preeminent source on this subject for the majority of Russian pianists. Because of his incredible influence on me (I studied under some of his pupils), his ideas will be encountered frequently in this book. His style of playing, his taste, and his many quotes – which have since turned into popular expressions – have all been imbedded in me since my youth. Additionally, in my approach to developing pianistic skills, I rely on the methods of the famous Russian teacher and healer, Anna Schmidt-Shklovskaya, whose exercises have for many years been widely used by Russian pedagogues. In this book readers will be presented with a strategy that allows for the mastering of pianistic techniques in the early stages to be natural and effective. These techniques will also prevent professional injuries. Each section that introduces a new technique contains a detailed explanation. The clarification is supported by accompanying musical examples in the form of musical exercises and pieces that make use of the new technique. The section dealing with the pianistic apparatus includes photographic illustrations, which should also aid in illuminating theoretical concepts.

Prominently appearing in this book is an artistically diverse musical repertoire, selected not solely for teaching piano, but also for helping cultivate the student's musical taste. As well as providing some interesting facts about their creators, the pieces are accompanied by colorful illustrations and short descriptions that will familiarize the child with the details surrounding the compositions. The book includes pieces from various eras, genres, and styles. These works are by composers who were highly skilled in writing for children. Alongside solo compositions are 4-hand pieces for student and teacher. Playing in any ensemble develops the ability to listen to your partner, as well as bringing a great deal of joy. In addition to popular pieces, the book's repertoire also includes music that is rarely performed and even undeservedly forgotten. This wonderful music should be given the opportunity to be heard more often. Editions used in the book are as close to the original as possible, and at times are the originals themselves. While keeping in mind the style of each composer, I have added necessary articulation, dynamic, and fingering markings in places where the composer did not supply them. The repertoire in the book can be used for the first six or seven years of study and should be of great help to students performing in recitals, festivals, and competitions.

Throughout my teaching career, I have had students with every conceivable problem and a wide range of musical involvement. In order to achieve a favorable pianistic result with such students, very detailed work on every component of piano-playing is required. However, a good musical result requires something more—the cultivation of musical culture. Perhaps what distinguishes the best of teachers is their ability to foster students in such a way that the pupils achieve brilliant pianism through a coalescence of their physical and spiritual developments. This requires the teacher to have an understanding not only of music but of art as a whole, including literature and the visual arts, while being willing to impart this knowledge to the student.

I never discriminate between promising and non-promising students; each child has his or her own speed of comprehension. One should never skimp on the resources necessary for any student's cultivation. There are known instances of *wunderkinds* abruptly stopping in their tracks of development and failing to become eminent performers, while ordinary students, benefitting from wise teachers, become spectacular musicians. We can never predict the future of a child, for whom a teacher takes great professional and personal responsibility from the very first lesson. In order for the study of music to make a valuable contribution to personal development, each student should be allowed to acquire his or her maximum amount of knowledge and skills. It is this conviction that has led to the creation of the book.

Developing Initial Musical Skills

On the Nature and Development of a Musical Ear

A musical ear, in a rudimentary sense, is present in each person, though the degree to which this ear is developed depends on many factors. Development is firstly linked to natural talent and secondly to experience. There was a time in Russia when the absence of a clearly-defined musical ear meant being denied acceptance to a music school. Later, educators came to the conclusion that such a system was flawed, as a musical sense lends itself to being intensively developed.

The idea of musical hearing may be broadly divided into two aspects: internal and external. The definition of the external is quite clear: It is the hearing that allows for the comprehension of the music currently being played. To listen with internal hearing means to imagine in one's mind the sound of a musical piece and to experience the same emotions as one would from actually hearing music. Another way of defining internal hearing is the ability to hear music by reading a score. Such hearing is incredibly developed in conductors, who often find it necessary to work with a score in the absence of an orchestra.

Why is internal hearing so important? Because playing on any musical instrument follows the "hear-reproduce" paradigm. The more detailed a musician's concept of what he or she is to play, the more precise the brain-commands that are sent to the hands, minimizing mistakes in performance.

Internal and external hearing abilities are undoubtedly interconnected. An underdeveloped skill in external hearing prevents any cultivation of the inner sense.

There is a well-known theory that a musical ear can be cultivated during the prenatal period of human life. In practice, this has been confirmed: The sooner a child is immersed in the sound-world of classical music, the sharper the musical ear, and the more naturally and easily he or she will be able to master a musical instrument and the complex language of classical music composers. It is not a coincidence that many offspring of musicians decide to follow in their parents' footsteps.

In order to develop the sense of inner hearing, it is essential to devote a portion of a lesson to exercises that stimulate melodic and harmonic comprehension in music. Singing different intervals out loud will assist in melodic development, i.e. it will help one know the exact distances between pitches. It is very important to show the intoned interval on the music stave so that the child may visually associate it with the sound. In order for a student to learn to identify intervals aurally, many teachers have traditionally associated the character of the sound with a particular animal. As an example, in melodic form, a third can be thought of as imitating the sound of a cuckoo, while a second, played in blocked form, reminds one of a hedgehog's needles. Composers often will use such imagery in composing children's character pieces.

Following singing intervals, teachers should start working with students on singing longer melodies. Not only does singing *solfège* help to improve the musical ear, but it is also instrumental in developing articulation in speech, which is intimately connected to finger articulation possibilities. Many children hum on a single note rather than sing, which does not necessarily indicate a lack of musicality, but rather an inability to control their vocal apparatus. This shortcoming will also be eliminated with continuous vocal exercises.

The successful singing of melodies, and the repetition of short, little songs on the piano, facilitates moving forward to the most difficult exercise – the musical dictation. Writing out a dictation demands close attention to listening to the melody, the ability to remember and reproduce the melody internally, and is very helpful in the practice of notation. At first, only the notes of the melody should be notated, without rhythms, so that the student can concentrate on one problem at a time. To remain manageable, the dictations should be very simple and short, and their complexity should increase only gradually. If the student is unable to identify the exact pitch, then he or she should be taught to analyze the shape of the melody by breaking it into smaller sections. This melody can be represented on paper as one uninterrupted line that changes direction together with the sound, either up or down. (The illustration resembles a cardiogram.) Following this, a more detailed blueprint of the melody's development would be indicated by determining where the melody moves by steps (scalar), and where there are skips (intervals larger than a second). Lastly, the student would concentrate on identifying the individual skips.

Recognizing intervals and chords played in blocked form improves one's harmonic sense. A harmonic sense is the ability to hear music vertically, distinguishing harmonic colors. Similar to associating intervals with animal imagery, it is possible to invent a chain of associations that would aid in the perception of each harmony as its own image.

One method I constantly use to invoke internal hearing while working with a student through a piece is the following: Play one hand on the piano, and the other hand on the upper part of the leg, while hearing this part internally. This method is both more difficult and more effective than simply practicing hands separately. It also trains rhythmic coordination between the hands.

On Rhythm

Rhythm is one of the most highly expressive resources in music. Like a musical ear, a sense of rhythm is universally innate. Even very small children are able to tap the beat of a melody quite rhythmically. When it comes to performance, however, a natural sense of rhythm is all too often insufficient. Rhythm, like musical hearing, demands intensive work; it can and should be developed.

I always explain to my students the difference between the rhythmic palette and the static heartbeat in music, so that they may clearly understand the concept of rhythm and meter. As Iser Slonim astutely observed, 'Meter is the skeleton of music; rhythm is its soul'.

A variety of games, such as exercises that involve combinations of movement, music, and words, can assist students in developing a sense of rhythm. A child can be shown the rhythmic notation of a familiar song. Together, recite the words while the child taps the rhythmic patterns upon a table, using his or her fingertips. Later, the exercise's level of difficulty can be increased by writing the song in two parts: the pulse in one hand and the full rhythmic pattern in the other. This is an excellent exercise for hand coordination.

Writing out rhythmic dictation also helps greatly in enhancing the sense of rhythm. While at first only using different combinations of quarter- and eighth-notes, I gradually increase the complexity of the rhythmic pattern.

In my experience, counting out loud while playing a piece is fruitless, since children will subject their counting to the movement of their hands, and not vice versa. Any type of technical difficulty will have an effect on the speed of vocal pronunciation. Moreover, counting out loud will prevent children from hearing the musical sound. It is far more effective to study the rhythmic pattern separately, away from the piano, by clapping the rhythm or tapping it with the fingertips on a surface. And, in a case where the student is away from the piano, counting out loud would be a helpful addition. Instead of simply counting the beats (1-and-2-and), I use the terminology of *Zoltán Kodály, in which every note-duration has its own name (ta-quarter, ti-eighth, etc.).*

In playing particularly difficult rhythmic sections, it can be helpful to have the students pronounce words or phrases that precisely correspond to the rhythmic pattern in question. A common example is the word triplet; pronounced *TRIP-uh-let*, it can help with the execution of its namesake rhythmic pattern.

I usually manage to avoid use of the metronome while improving a student's abilities to feel a steady pulse. Instead of using an inanimate object that kills breath in music, I prefer to give my students a conducting baton, which helps them independently feel the pulse. Conducting does not only develop a sense of meter in a child, but it also exercises the flowing movement of the arm, which is crucial to piano-playing.

A short lesson on introductory conducting technique:

(The hand moves from beat to beat in a gentle, arch-like movement, using the entire arm).

Duple pattern: Begin with a high position of the hand. On beat one, the hand moves down; on beat two, it returns upward.

Triple pattern: Begin as in the duple pattern. The hand moves down, to the right, and back up, as if drawing a triangle in the air.

Quadruple pattern: The hand moves down, left, right, and back up.

Preparatory Stages

One of the main problems in the early stages of learning musical instrument is playing from printed music. A child that is unprepared for music lessons will be overwhelmed in trying to solve the puzzle of multitasking: identifying the notes, quickly finding the right key, and maintaining control over the hands and the sound. An easier teaching method exists. This method is based on studying pieces written on the principle of a five-finger position, in which each key corresponds to only one finger. I do not deny the usefulness of such pieces when used within the overall repertoire. My collection includes the pieces of Maykapar and Cui, in which the student's part is structured on the five-finger formula. Nevertheless, I must call for a balanced approach. A beginner's repertoire should not be limited to such pieces, as the result may be deceptive. The problem, in this case, is that the student would learn the piece not based on the actual notes on the stave, but rather by following the fingerings. This may be a comfortable and easy method, but also an anti-musical, dead-end approach that would limit the student's future technical and artistic capabilities.

There is yet another method that lays a foundation for piano-playing and score-reading and leads to professional results. This method includes a preparatory period dedicated to singing intervals and short melodies, developing rhythm, studying the keyboard, and thoroughly working on developing the pianistic apparatus. The synthesis of these skills will transition to playing short melodies by ear (it is best to use only the second or third finger). Concurrently, the position of the notes on the stave can be memorized. It is essential to analyze the printed note's correlation to the key, so that the child can understand the logic behind the notation. While developing a sense of pitch, it is vital to connect each sound to its corresponding key on the piano and the note on the stave. Teaching students to read music can be accomplished through a variety of helpful games, including music theory flash cards, music notation computer software, and other learning materials that transform learning into fun. Learning to read music by practicing on a daily basis will yield results quickly. Parents should be aware that it is impossible to learn to read music only in lessons; most of the work takes place at home.

Much attention during this stage should be directed towards developing musical horizons by acquiring listening and analytical skills. For this, the teacher may consult the *Dance Voyage* and *Children's Albums* sections of this book, where musical excerpts are accompanied by historical overviews and illustrations.

Every child is unique in the amount of talent or work ethic. This fact prohibits any precise instruction as to how long this preparatory period should last. For me, a student's ability to confidently play simple pieces using *non legato*, obtain a pianistic hand, move the arms freely, be oriented on the keyboard, and be able to read music within a two-octave range, signifies that he or she is ready to play from a score. At that point, all of these skills can be assembled to aid in score-reading.

Sight-Reading

Sight-reading is the visual identification of a printed note or symbol, the inner hearing of that note, and the immediate transfer of the seen and heard note to the hand muscles. It is a highly-complex process that involves vision, hearing, and motor skills. Not everyone is able to fully develop all of these components and successfully integrate them into one action. For that reason, at times even very gifted children will find sight-reading to be very challenging. Only experience can help.

An important requirement for effectively learning to sight-read is that the printed notes are large enough to see. Moreover, the placement of the score on the music desk is significant: The closer the score is to the hands, the easier it becomes to simultaneously see the music as well as the keyboard's layout.

However sight-reading does require the skill of playing blindly. More than anything else, this frightens beginner pianists. The eyes of a child are involuntarily focused on the hands, in the same way that a beginner cyclist will focus on the feet and pedals, as opposed to the road ahead. It is difficult to teach a child not to be tempted to look at the hands. Usually, I will hold a piece of paper above the hands during sight-reading.

A few practical pieces of advice to teachers:

1. Ask the student to sing a melody in *solfège* while playing an easy sight-reading piece, developing the connection between the visual representation and the aural.

2. Make sure that the repertoire used for sight-reading is chosen according to the student's abilities. For sight-reading, beginners use the "five-finger position" songs, which don't require hand shifting. Gradually increase the complexity of the musical fabric, moving from patterned melodies to more advanced material.

3. Using easy double-voiced pieces, such as Bartók's *Mikrokosmos*, ask the student to play one voice and sing the other.

4. Teach your students to quickly memorize what they are seeing. Choose a very simple piece. Ask the student to look at the first measure and then play it by memory. Repeat the process with the next measure and eventually increase the selections to be memorized.

5. During sight-reading cover the note or, better, the whole motive that is to be played at that moment. This will stimulate the student to always look ahead.

6. In sight-reading, aside from a good set of motor skills, it is also vital to use correct fingering. This skill will accumulate with experience: The larger the repertoire, the faster the hands will remember common fingerings. Using short melodies, based on specific technical ideas, exercise the student's abilities to use desired finger patterns.

7. Motivate the student to sight-read every day.

The Means of Expression in Performance

If a child can reproduce the simplest of melodies, it is crucial to make sure this initial 'performance' is done expressively, namely that the character of the performance matches the character of the melody.

Heinrich Neuhaus

Working with students on the artistic facets of a musical composition reminds me of filling in black and white drawings with color. In order for a piece to be enlivened through color, sound closer to the composer's vision, and penetrate the soul of the listener, much work is needed both on the emotional state of the performer, and on each of the musical and pianistic devices employed for expressivity.

Sound Production

Music is the art of sound.

Heinrich Neuhaus

I am often asked what the chief tenet of the Russian School of piano pedagogy is. There isn't a single answer to this question, as every musician has his or her own tastes and methods. There is, however, certainly an overall sense of tradition. The high concentration of eminent Russian artist-teachers in the first half of the twentieth century led to the formation of certain ideas, which have been passed on through the generations. One of these concepts is the importance of instilling the student with a love for the piano sound.

Sometimes, the lack of demand for a quality sound stems from the assertion that children aren't capable of interesting sound production. *Demand the impossible from your student, so that you may get the desirable* – the advice of Heinrich Neuhaus. In my experience, these words ring true even for children who are not extraordinarily talented in music. When children are taught visual art, they are necessarily told about colors, warm and cool shades, color combinations, and color mixes that create new shades. By contrast, when it comes to musical lessons, too often teachers become so preoccupied with the mechanics of depressing a key that they forget about what matters most – the result of that key depression. Naturally, one cannot expect a variety of timbral shadings from a beginner, but it is certainly realistic to teach high-quality sound that stays within the boundaries of what musicians call "not-yet-sound" (insufficient key depression that does not allow the hammer to fully activate all of the strings associated with it) and "no-longer-sound" (when a key is hit harshly, producing an open, colorless sound).

Working on sound consists primarily of intensive listening to a sound until the very moment of its end, and a controlled transition into the following sound. Concentrating on these actions will not only improve the quality of the sound, but will also help prevent the possibility of any extra-musical distraction during performance. Sound production must be predicated by sound anticipation—internally imagining the sound. When internal listening skills are honed and the musical imagination is encouraged to include a refined idea of what should sound and how, the chances that the sound will be interesting increase. However, even a precise understanding of the musical character and an inner realization of the sonoral atmosphere might be insufficient. In order to realize the internally-heard sound, it is essential to find the necessary physical sensation in the hands and fingers, as the sound depends upon the manner in which they touch the keyboard. Experienced performers will intuitively exert necessary movements, subjecting the hands' actions to the musical concept. By contrast, to children, who have not yet fully developed their pianistic capabilities, it is important to explain the physical sensations in the hands and fingers, and the centrality of connecting those sensations to the necessary movements.

For the sake of building associations and developing aural imagery, it is useful to invoke the various tonal colors of different instruments. This is especially helpful for differentiating colors of voices in polyphony. Likewise, it is important to stimulate an interest in listening to recordings of great performers, expanding the student's perception of the piano's sound palette.

Dynamics

Working on sound includes acquiring the skill for using variable dynamics. The chief dynamic markings of *forte* and *piano* ought to be used in the very first pieces of study. One should not expect a child to produce a full-bodied *forte* sound at the outset, much as we wouldn't expect a mighty operatic singing voice from a child. Playing in true *piano* requires precision work, even for experienced performers. Children typically will lack timbral color in their sound if attempting to play too softly. The main goal in the early stages of study should be achieving dynamic contrast between phrases.

Forte: Playing with a full-bodied sound is only possible with the use of the full arm's weight and the energy transferred through the torso's movement. Children are prone to tense their muscles specifically with the goal of playing louder. A child may involuntarily believe that he or she must exert more effort to achieve a louder sound. Playing loudly with a tense hand is not only ineffective, but it is also physically dangerous – muscle injury from fatigue could occur. One essential physical rule is that the faster the arm drops and the more relaxed the muscles at the moment of key depression, the louder the resulting sound. Feeling the use of the full arm from the shoulder, with a relaxed upper arm, is essential.

Piano: The closer the finger is to the key and the less arm weight used, the softer the sound. Playing quietly is difficult, as there is always a danger of not reaching the point of sound. Children will associate the softness of sound with the softness of their fingers, which, in soft playing, are often in a state I call "noodley." Even when we use less-curved fingers in lyrical music, the distal phalanx should never lose its form, allowing for the very tip of the finger to come in contact with the key. While playing in *piano*, the fingers should be especially active, with a sense of "reaching" for the sound from the bottom of the keyboard.

In producing different dynamics, it is pertinent to remember the particularities of the piano's construction. The highest register always requires very intensive touch, even if the music is marked *pianissimo*. Analogously, in the low register, we must limit the weight of the arm and use a very gentle touch.

18

It is best to introduce more complicated dynamic markings (such as *cresc. and dim.*) when a repertoire contains pieces that use *legato* in the melody. Students will often equate *cresc.* with *forte*, and will mistake *piano* for *dim*. On the contrary, these are markings of growth and subsidence, advancing and receding. To help a student to implement a correct dynamic in performance, I usually include further instructions in the music:

Crescendo – start softly and gradually increase the level of sound.

Diminuendo – begin louder and gradually reduce the level of sound.

Dynamics in a score are not simply indicators of the level of volume. Quite often, dynamic markings are more indicative of the character and atmosphere of music. Thus, *piano* may be an indication of calm that nevertheless requires a deep and full sound (see Tchaikovsky's *Old French Song*). Similarly, *forte* can point less to a purely loud sonority, instead indicating a joyful spirit or energy (see Schumann's *Happy Farmer*).

In working out a piece of music, it is important to achieve a dynamic balance between the melody and accompaniment, and between the various voices of a polyphonic composition. Success in this depends on the level of development in discerning aural capabilities, which are necessary to evenly distribute control throughout the various components of the musical texture. Introductory work on sonoral balance should be composed of simple material. Teachers should consider, for their young students, including easy, double-voiced pieces in the repertoire, as well as ones that clearly distinguish between melody and accompaniment. It is important to note that although a dynamic marking appears as a single value, the musical texture is in fact multi-layered. For each part of the musical texture to sound clearly, it is necessary to find its own corresponding dynamics.

Sweet Dream

Moderato

Pyotr Thaikovsky

In the above example the upper voice is performed legato with a singing tone. Although the overall dynamic marking in the selection is piano, the upper voice should ring out above the other layers of the texture. In order for the sound to soar, the touch employed should be quite vigorous (deep), using full arm, as the melody is written in a high register. One might imagine that the part of the right hand is played by a violin.

The left hand separated into low bass notes and intervallic jumps. The movement of the bass line corresponds with the movement of the upper voice, which is executed by the right hand. Dynamically, the low voice should be played softly, as it is written in the low register; otherwise, it would overpower the melody. Physically, the left hand should feel as if it is performing two independent functions: The first is responsible for the bass line, played by moving with the arm firmly into the bottom of the key in order to invoke a deep, cello-like sound; the second is responsible for the intervallic jumps, which should be played piano by lightly grasping the keys with the tips of the fingers and moving "out" of the keyboard.

Realizations of dynamic markings also depend on the individual styles of composers. For example, a *forte* in Mozart is different from a *forte* in Beethoven. The diversity in the usage of dynamics among various composers is associated with the piano's growing scope of sonoral capabilities, as well as with the general development of musical language. In contemporary compositions, it is possible to encounter dynamic indications of *ffffff* or *pppp*, which would be difficult to imagine in nineteenth-century compositions. Nevertheless, the master of instructional studies, Carl Czerny, had in his day already concluded that the piano is capable of one-hundred different gradations of dynamics.

The Art of Phrasing

The melody is not a projection of successive notes; it is carefully and consistently built up of melodic-units, each of them independent, yet all dependent on each other, and calling for various degrees of rhythmic and emotional accentuation.

Leopold Auer

Music is a language. Likewise literary work, musical composition contains a predetermined structure that includes motives, phrases, sentences, periods, and sections. These, in turn, form other, larger structural divisions.

A line of music is divided into bars in accordance with a meter, which is not connected with music's logical progression. This often confuses children. In the preliminary stages, having dismantled the barriers of the bar line, the student should be introduced to the shortest of structures: a sentence, a phrase, a motive. A **musical sentence** is a complete thought, which in musical terms can be identified as ending with a cadence. A sentence is divided into 2-3 **phrases**, each of which is further divided into motives. A **motive** is the smallest part of a musical thought. As any tissue or fabric is made up of cells, a musical fabric is composed of motives.

The ability to break down a long musical phrase into motives often alleviates technical and rhythmic difficulties, particularly in cases where the musical structure of the phrase corresponds to a desirable technical grouping. Usually, this occurs in instructional *études*:

Study

Allegro moderato

Ludwig Shitte

In this example, achieving clarity and evenness in the passagework at a fast tempo is only possible if the melody is broken into groupings that are performed with one unifying movement. If the division into motives begins from the first note, creating groups of four notes each, then the interval of a third between the first and second notes prevents a smooth motion of the wrist. Therefore, it is best to begin the grouping from the second note, which is played with a sense of support. The other notes in the group are played more lightly, using a single motion of the forearm and leading up to the final note of the motive. That final note acts as the physical and rhythmic fulcrum, as well as the moment of tension release. This method of grouping will aid in playing the melodic line in a rhythmically stable, even, and clear mode.

Aside from having a structure like prose, music can be associated with poetry because of its high emotional impact and expressiveness of declamation. Children with underdeveloped musical awareness lack an intuitive sense for musical phrasing. Once again, a parallel can be made here with linguistics. Foreign students studying the English language typically make one of two mistakes: They will either unnecessarily underscore each word, or will pronounce all words monotonously. That is precisely the way students who are not taught to unify sounds into groups or to feel the tonal tension of a phrase perform music. Contrary to spoken languages, where certain key words may suffice in finding the sentence's meaning by way of vocally stressing those words, music is abstract, and its expressive qualities (phrasing) cannot be easily found, by a beginner, from context alone.

I usually find a word or a combination of words, that coincides with the motive or phrase in question and verbalize it to a student, indicating the required inflection or stress. For example, every cadence that involves resolving a dissonance into a consonance on a weak beat can be represented by a two-syllable word with the stress on the first syllable (children practically always play just the opposite, with the stress on the resolution.)

It is essential to remember breaths, those unnoticeable gaps between phrases and sentences that aid in showing the ends of musical thoughts more clearly. I usually draw a parallel with singers, for whom it is a physical necessity to take a breath in predetermined spots. The sense of breathing should also be manifested in the hands, allowing for a natural movement to symbolize minuscule stops in the musical speech. For children, it is essential to learn to "come off" the keyboard in moments of breath, while moving smoothly in the direction of the following phrase.

The end of a musical thought as well as a specific musical character can be expressed by inserting punctuation marks, such as commas, periods, question marks, and exclamation marks, in between phrases.

Waltz

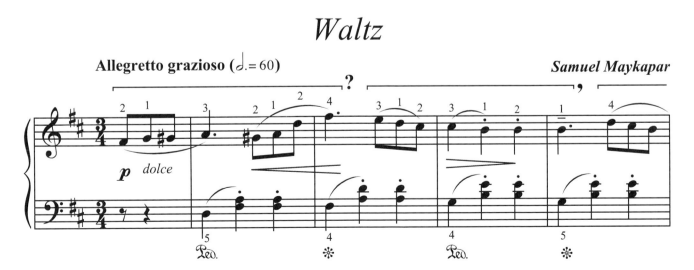

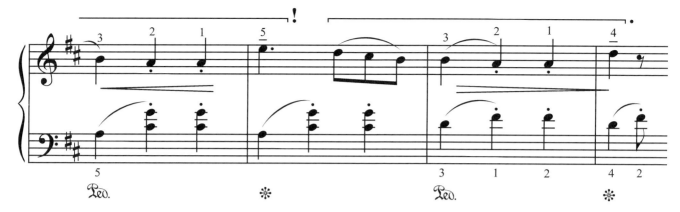

I also use "*cresc.*" and "*dim.*" within individual motives or phrases. These signs can help the student imagine minute dynamic changes in the sound, symbolizing the altered pitch of the human voice, which would be impossible for composers or editors to include in standard notation and would make a performance more personal and expressive.

Sustain Pedal

Good pedaling – three quarters of good piano-playing.

A. Rubinstein

The sustain pedal should only be used once the student has learned to listen to his or her own self and to consciously control the transfer from one sound to the next.

It is important that pedaling be comfortable. If the student is unable to physically reach the pedals, then a pedal extender should be used. Prior to connecting the actions of the feet and the hands, proper pedal contact should be established. The foot ought to be firmly grounded on the floor with the heel, and should come in contact with the wider part of the pedal with roughly one-third of the foot. It is important to get used to feeling as if the foot is fused with the pedal, as opposed to simply hitting it from above.

While the pedal is never pressed all the way down, there are such concepts as half-pedal and quarter-pedal. The more frequently the pedal is used, the less deeply it should be pressed. The pressing and releasing movements can be slow or quick, depending on the goal. If a complete clearing of the previous harmony is desired, the pedal should be changed slowly.

There are two basic pedaling concepts: direct and delayed. Direct pedaling, also referred to as rhythmic pedaling, and involves pressing the pedal together with a new sound and releasing it before playing the next one. Children easily grasp this type of pedaling. Delayed pedaling (when the pedal is pressed after playing a note and released while playing a next one) is used far more often, and it is also more difficult. As a preparatory exercise for delayed pedaling, I often make use of a simple scale. As soon as the student is able to synchronize the movement of the fingers with the foot, this type of pedaling can begin to be used in pieces.

In the beginning stages, direct pedaling is used in pieces that have a well-defined rhythmic element (Schumann's *Soldier's March*) and delayed pedaling in pieces where the harmonies change slowly – no faster than once per measure (Tchaikovsky's *Sick Doll*; Sviridov's *Gentle Request*). Later on, as the student acquires certain abilities, the pedal begins to play a more diverse and complex role: for a *legato* effect in cases where the hands alone cannot achieve it; for enhancing dynamics; and for tone-color effects.

As is the case with our fingers, the pedal should be guided by the ear, as well as by knowledge and experience. Pedal changes usually occur so often and in so many ways that composers and editors cannot always give precise pedaling indications. The use of the pedal depends on many factors, including the composer's individual style, the particular abilities of different pianos, and the effect it would have on the room's acoustics. It becomes a teacher's responsibility to provide student with detailed pedal instructions. For a remarkable textbook on pedaling, I can recommend Maykapar's *20 Pedal Preludes*, whereby the principles of piano pedaling are explored through pieces that gradually increase in difficulty.

Developing Fundamentals of Piano Technique

Should any great musician be asked to define technique, the answer would always be along the same lines: While the ultimate goal of performance is the musician's blossoming of the composer's artistic seed, technique is the means whereby this musical bloom can come to fruition. This "means" requires a significant investment. Just as the ballerina must learn an arsenal of movements at the bar prior to learning a dance, the beginning pianist, too, must acquire an essential collection of different pianistic movements.

The Nature of Pianistic Movements

A physical justification exists for all gestures employed in piano-playing. If a sound's origin is within the mind, then the entire body must be its actuator – from the pelvis through the spine, into the arms and out through the fingertips. All of the components of the arm act together in fulfilling the brain's command. Each part of the arm has its unique function, but collectively they compose a full apparatus, or instrument.

If one were to examine the work of a painter, it would become apparent that even short strokes upon the canvas employ the use of the full arm, which allows an artist to work for hours without feeling strain. Likewise, if we specifically analyze any delicate actions performed regularly, such as threading a needle, or, conversely, if we scrutinize intensive ones, such as cleaning a window, we will notice that they are carried out using the large muscles of the arm. These large muscles are what prevent us from overexerting our wrists and fingers when we perform precise and quick movements. Therefore, in the early stages of learning, the development of good finger articulation should not be the primary goal. Preference should be given to mastering the skills of using the large muscles, creating a foundation for good pianistic health. Later on, once this foundational basis is secure, developing a virtuosic technique of the small muscles will be more effective and will make us less prone to injury or hypertension. This is the underlying principle for the section of the book dealing with exercises and pieces for the development of technical skills. The techniques used in these exercises lead, over time, to the proper engagement of the small and large parts of the pianistic apparatus, laying out a foundation for the successful future development of piano technique.

Any movement that a novice pianist performs amounts to a new physical experience for them. In order for the movement to become habitual and comfortable, it is essential to precede any new technical skill with extra-pianistic exercises that help to work on the new movement. While the student performs these exercises, it is easier for the teacher to assess the unique build and capabilities of the student's hand. This book contains examples of such exercises that I use in my own practice.

Quite often, a child will discover unique playing movements that best fit his or her particular set of hands; those same movements will yield favorable results when they are executed on the piano. Even if these movements do not follow the "rules," the student should not be prevented from using such unique movements as any forced deviation from them would only be detrimental. Likewise, it would disadvantageous to attempt to change students' hand positions who may have not been properly taught, but who have nevertheless been playing for a while. Any physical discrepancies should be corrected slowly and carefully, while minute errors are at times best not corrected at all.

Teachers should not overlook the importance of controlling extraneous movements. Children sometimes move their body to an exaggerated degree, allowing the "pathos" of their movement to influence their performance. If great musicians are able to manipulate the character of their sound by way of informed movement, then children who imitate them without any musical justification would conversely stand to ruin the sound. Unnatural movements of the body, as well as exaggerated lifts of the arms, are prime reasons for loss of control at the keyboard. A well thought out design for movement will contribute to better sound production, rhythm, articulation, and the synchronization of the two hands.

Tension and Relaxation

It is vital to understand the key physical principle in piano-playing – successful performance is achieved when musicians alternate between controlled muscular tension and relaxation. Relaxation is crucial for preventing playing-related injuries caused by hypertension.

The following exercise will help a child to understand the feeling of controlled tension and relaxation:

"Airplane:" With the arms outstretched to the sides like the wings of an airplane, lean forward, bending at the waist until your torso is parallel to the floor; maintain this position for a few seconds, and then release the arms, allowing them to naturally swing from side to side.

Tension may also be involuntary, arising from the inability to control one's muscle state. One example of this is raising the shoulders while playing.

As an exercise, it is recommended that the student raise and lower his or her shoulders, maintaining each position for a number of seconds, so that both correct and incorrect positions may be consciously observed.

Exercises for Muscular Relaxation

The following exercises are best performed during rest periods, in between practice sessions:

1. **"Morning stretches:"** Begin with a slightly arched torso. On the inhale, rise on your toes while simultaneously and gently lifting your arms up above your head, crossing your fingers at the top and then stretching your arms out to the sides. On the exhale, while your body returns to its slightly curved position, allow your arms to completely relax and drop down, swinging freely until all motion ceases.

2. **"A Treadmill:"** The full body is relaxed. Rotate each arm from the shoulder joint, singly at first and then together, forward and backward. In this exercise, it is important to maintain a relaxed arm throughout, as the goal is not to develop muscle strength but to be able to use the muscles in a relaxed state.

3. **"Arm Drop:"** The student sits on a chair with the hands hanging freely. Taking the wrist, the teacher lifts the student's arm up, asking the student to relax his or her arm fully. The teacher then lets go of

the arm. If the arm remains in the high position, then the muscles are tense. The desirable relaxed state is one in which the arm drops down freely after being let go.

Position at the Piano

A proper position at the piano requires careful attention. One should sit at the piano in such a way that it is comfortable to move the hands, with full control, along the entire length of the keyboard. Here are some general rules for beginning pianists that should be adhered to in the first few years:

1. The pianist is situated in front of the middle octave of the keyboard, the markers generally being D^4-E^4.

2. The distance between the piano and the player should be such that the elbows, slightly moved to the sides, are lined up with the torso, or are slightly in front of it.

3. The sitting height should be determined by a straight line from the wrist to the elbows, with the forearms, which ought to be on the same plane as the keyboard, slightly moved away from the torso. A very low or very high wrist is usually an indicator of an incorrect sitting height.

4. The pianist should sit on the front half of the piano bench, with feet firmly planted on the floor. This is why it is so important to place a supporting footrest under the feet of young children, so that their feet do not dangle freely in the air. This support will also eliminate tension in the hips. With freely dangling feet, a child is prone to lean backward, depriving the body of a full sense of support and control at the keyboard. A lack of support in the feet also contributes to spine problems, as the back will tend to arch. All of this influences the arms, which are dependent on the back muscles for their movement.

5. It is equally important to take note of the student's visual abilities. A child should be comfortably able to see a score. When working with young children, it may be more favorable to work at an upright piano instead of a grand, with the music desk of the upright being lower and closer both to the eyes and the hands. If the music desk is too high, the head will tend to strain upwards, causing tension to the neck muscles.

With age and experience, each musician will find his or her most effective and optimal position at the piano.

Establishing Contact with Keyboard

Hand Position

Human hands have a natural tendency to maintain a slightly curved pianistic position. However, as soon as contact is established with the key, everything begins to fail due to incorrect weight distribution and inept movements. The form of the hand is very important: The back of the hand should not be depressed (collapsed) or tight. Just as our feet are naturally dome-shaped (arched), allowing them to withstand great pressure, our hands must also maintain a dome-shaped position during playing. This is especially important to establish in novice players so that they will be prepared when their repertoire expands to become filled with works that demand stretching of the hand and a powerful sound. It is reliance on the palm muscles, achievable with the dome shape, that will help prevent any overstressing of the wrist and fingers that might lead to professional injury.

A skilful performer would analyze, perceive, and control the optimal hand movement along the keyboard. The purpose of the hand movement is to assure the most comfortable position for the effective working of the fingers. Fingers must be above the keys (without touching them) slightly ahead of time to ensure the desired type of touch will happen at exactly the right moment. It is especially important for achieving evenness of tone while performing a melody with large intervals, shifts of hand position, or jumps.

Such hand movement is in turn facilitated by the action of both the arm and the wrist. The arm is responsible for large, unifying movements, while the wrist does the "fine-tuning" with more delicate action, while following the melody line and working in cooperation with the fingers. It is acting as kind of a bridge connecting the hand with the forearm. Care should be taken for this "bridge" to be flexible, resilient, and efficient in its movement as well as sturdy when necessary. An overly loosened state of the wrist (usually resulting from the lack of the fingers' activity) leads to technical and sonoral problems, while never relaxing the wrist (playing with isolated fingers) may lead to injuries.

Touching the Keyboard

Prior to approaching the piano, a young student should be aware that we do not strike the keys; rather, we come into contact with them by way of touch. We carry out this touch with our fingertip. The tip of the finger should be in a constant state of heightened sensitivity. **A firm grip of the fingertip on the key essential for quality sound production**. With the achievement of proper contact with the key, or, in other words, with the feeling of "grabbing" the key with the fingertip, the problem of a caved-in distal phalanx disappears, and the dome-shaped hand position is restored. In order for the child to understand exactly what point of the finger should come in contact with the key, a dot may be marked on the finger, using a pen. For proper sensation of the fingertips, the following exercises are useful:

Put the hands together, with the fingertips of each pair of fingers pressing against one another. In turn, tap each pair of fingertips together.

The sensation of "grabbing" the key with the fingertip may be demonstrated through the following:

The student places the forearm on the table, the hand supported on the fingertips. The student rubs the tip of each finger, without losing contact with the surface.

The absence of fingertip-to-key grasping skills, and, as a consequence, the deformation of the fingers (collapsed phalanx, over-straightened fingers) negatively affects the position of the fingers on the keyboard. Fingers come into contact with the keys at their very edges when they ought to be aiming for the center, closer to the position of the black keys. This error leads to an incorrect wrist position, whereby the wrist drops below the level of the piano keys. Problems can also occur with the thumb, which will hang off the keys in this hand position, creating further technical problems.

A non-varied repertoire may also result in the tendency to play at the edge of the keyboard. Much of the teaching material for beginners is composed in C major, which does not utilize the black keys. Chopin's method of teaching beginners is helpful here. In order for his pupils to feel the keys at their most comfortable distribution, he would assign a simple five-finger pattern, to be played *non legato*, consisting of a portion of the B major scale (E, F#, G#, A#, B). In assigning a pattern such as this, the students would find that their shorter fingers were positioned on the white keys and the longer ones on the black keys. This natural positioning for the hand guaranteed the correct form for the fingers, and secured a basic comprehension of the alternating black-and-white nature of the piano keyboard. Using Chopin's formula may not always be effective, especially when dealing with very small hands, but it is essential to utilize beginner repertoire that contains accidentals.

Exercises and Pieces for the Third Finger

(Articulation: Non Legato; Staccato)

In order for beginners to become familiarized with the keyboard and navigate it freely, it is necessary that, during sound production, they feel the fingers pulled down, by gravity, into the key-bed. Therefore, when first establishing contact with the instrument, it is best to play *non legato*, dropping the arm from above. The arms of the professional pianist move in a variety of circular and vertical gestures. The forearms of poorly taught

students are limited to strictly horizontal movement from key to key, in which they avoid any kind of lift above the keyboard. This type of playing quickly tires the muscles and prevents technical mastery. Arced movements of the arm, which are used in preliminary piano exercises, facilitate a sense of freedom in one's movement upon the keyboard, and allow the use of the full arm. At first, these movements are exaggerated, but later on, they become less noticeable.

The first sound should be fashioned using a smooth, preparatory upward movement of the arm, in order to acquire enough downward momentum for the finger to freely fall into the keyboard. The starting position for an upward movement should be with the hand resting with the fingertips on the keyboard. The elbow should initiate the movement, akin to the flap of a wing; it should guide the forearm and lift the hand off the keyboard. The wrist should be relaxed, with the fingers pointing down. The movement should be slightly pointed in the direction of the keyboard lid. There is no need to lift the hand too high up. Instead, the motion should also be used to develop a sense of "breath" in the hand, necessary for expressive phrasing and physical relaxation.

The movement back down should be confident and precise. The downward movement should depend on the state of the arm muscles. The arm must be flexed: It should not be overly tensed, but neither should it be fully relaxed, or it would just hang by the weight of its muscles, like a hose. Initially, the teacher ought to control the state of the student's muscles, since the student does not yet know how to observe muscular behavior in the unfamiliar situation of having to hold the weight of the full arm. For a child, this task may become easier if the teacher helps hold the weight of the arm by gently supporting the student's elbow, while also preventing the elbow from touching the body. Once the finger is immersed in the key, it is important for the student to listen to the produced sound until it fully decays. No additional pressure should be placed on the key. Then, the teacher should ensure that the student smoothly transfers the hand with the help of the arm to the next sound, making a semi-circular shape in the air. During the transfer of the hand, it will help the student to imagine the sound itself being transferred. Teachers should confirm that the student's arm moves all the way from the shoulder and the finger presses the center of a key (the thumb should be above the keyboard and not below, as is often the case when playing near the edge of the keyboard). Additionally, teachers should encourage students to pay attention to their inactive fingers, which must be relaxed.

Many children engage the fingers with far too much pressure during *non legato* playing. Aside from that, *non legato* articulation alone does not aid in the development of fingertip sensitivity. Therefore, it is advisable to include *staccato* articulation (with a help of the arm) together with *non legato*. *Staccato* playing activates the fingers' briskness. As with *non legato* playing, the arm is engaged from the shoulder. Using light, active, and elastic movement, the fingertip "grabs" the key. The upward rebound motion should feel as if the key itself has pushed the finger out together with the hand, which "floats" to the next key, making a semi-circular shape in the air.

The following exercise helps to establish the proper movement of the arm:

"Rainbow:" Sitting at the middle of the keyboard, station the fingers on the keys in a cupped position. Using the support of the full arm, transfer both hands simultaneously to the opposite edges of the keyboard, as if drawing a rainbow in the air through the movement. In the same manner, bring the hands back together to the center.

All of the following exercises should be first practiced hands separately, and then with hands together.

Exercise 1

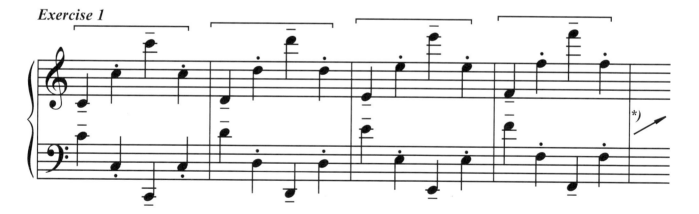

*) *Continue the sequence*

Exercise 2

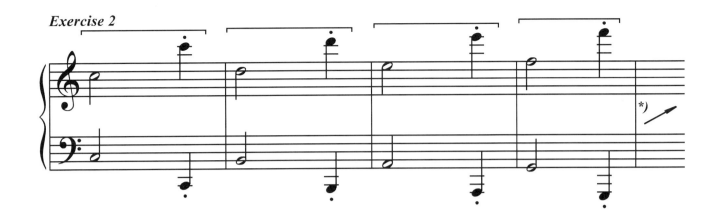

Exercise 3

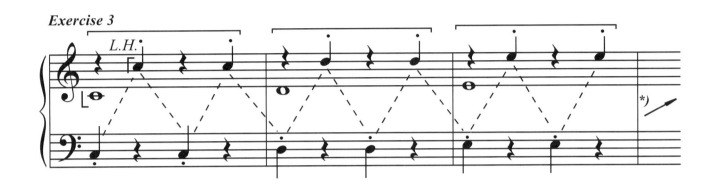

Exercise 4

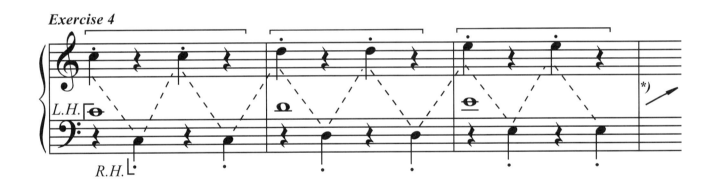

Exercise 5

*) Continue the sequence

Hello!

Blooming Tree

Hot Cross Bun

Black Keys

Paraphrases

One day, the young daughter of the famous Russian composer, Alexander Borodin, asked her father to play four-hands on the piano with her.

"But, dear," he said, "you don't really know how to play anything".

"Not true! Look, I can play this".

"She then played a very simple little tune for her father, using only one finger for each hand.

Conceding to the child's request, Borodin took the tune and, improvising on it, composed a unique and lively polka. He showed this improvisation to his friends, composers Rimsky-Korsakov and Lyadov. They laughed heartily and likewise attempted to compose some variations on this quite unchangeable theme. Cesar Cui soon took part as well. The results of this game were twenty-four variations and fourteen small pieces for the piano, published under the title Paraphrases.

Polka

Alexander Borodin
(1833 – 1887)

Minuet

Nikolay Rimsky-Korsakov
(1844 – 1908)

Exercises and Pieces Using the Second and Fourth Fingers

(Articulation: Non Legato; Staccato)

The index finger should be positioned in such a way that playing with it is fairly easy, while the fourth finger is the weakest and least independent of all. It is useful to play exercises not only on white keys, but on black keys as well. For a young student, the black keys not only discourage finger over-exertion, but also help secure the hand and position the fingertip for precise contact with the key.

Double-note exercises that employ the second and fourth fingers promote a hand position that allows the fourth finger to feel stable on the keyboard.

All of the following exercises should be first practiced hands separately, and then with hands together.

*) Continue the sequence

Theme from Variations

Wolfgang Amadeus Mozart
(1756 – 1791)

36

The Thumb

The first finger plays a crucial role in piano-playing. Because of its central part in this art form, this finger is sometimes referred to as the axis, or pivot, of the playing apparatus; as such, it must be given a great deal of attention.

The thumb (first finger), despite its short length and stubby width, is, in fact, physiologically the most independent finger. A thoroughly worked out thumb moves effortlessly and naturally. In poorly trained children, the thumb often exhibits a tendency to over-straighten and to lie on the full length of its side upon the key, leading unfortunately to the lowering of the wrist at the moment of key depression, as well as creating an undesirably harsh sound. The thumb should engage the key lightly, using the fleshy part of the finger right beside the nail. This amount of finger contact will suffice for depressing the key without any unnecessary downward movements, which cause a sunken wrist. The thumb's form should be such that, in the most basic position of the hand on the keyboard, a ring would be formed between the thumb and the index finger.

The thumb is typically responsible for a lack of evenness in difficult runs or in passages that require quick shifts in hand positions, using the finger combinations 2-1, 3-1, and 4-1. The actions of the thumb during changes of position are directly dependent on the position of the elbow, which should lead the forearm in the direction of the melody and turn the hand in such a way that the thumb arrives at the key before the moment of depression. This ensures the conditions for sound production through an exact and light touch.

Thumb Exercises Away from the Piano

1. **"Drawing Circles:"** Rotate a slightly-bent thumb clockwise and counterclockwise.
2. **"Cat and Little Bird:"** The student rests the forearm on the table (up to the elbow) and stands the hand on the fingers (this is the little birdhouse). The thumb is in a natural state (the bird is outside the house). The teacher depicts, using his or her fingers, a slowly-approaching cat, counting to three. On

the count of three, the student quickly hides the thumb underneath the palm (the bird hides away), and immediately relaxes the thumb. Repeat several times.

3. **"Rolling Play-Doh:"** Using the finger combinations 1-2, 1-3, and 1-4, make circular movements between each pair of touching fingertips, as if rolling a small ball of Play-Doh.

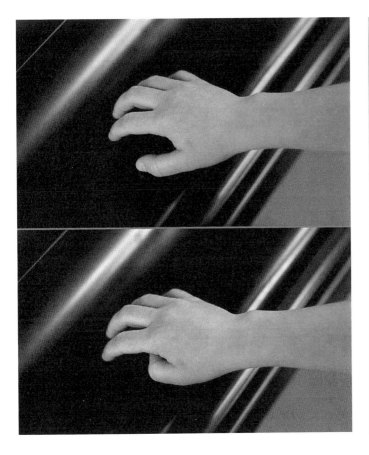

"Cat and Little Bird"   *"Rolling Play-Doh"*

All of the following exercises should be first practiced hands separately, and then with hands together.

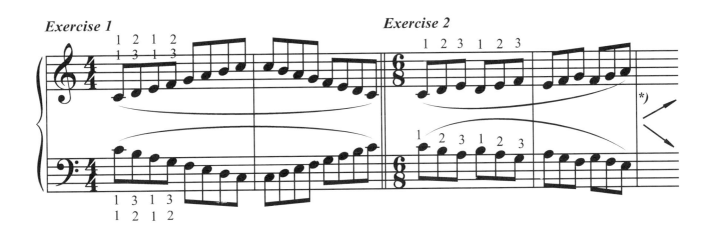

Exercise 3   *Exercise 4*

Exercise 5   *Exercise 6*

*) *Continue the sequence*

The Fifth Finger

The fifth finger carries a great burden in piano-playing: In the left hand it often leads the bass line, while in the right it is responsible for the melodic line. As a leading finger, it is necessary for it to be strengthened, which will happen over time. It is difficult, at first, to independently control the fifth finger, since in order to touch the key using the fingertip it is first necessary to find the correct position of the elbow; this formation helps to place the forearm and hand at the proper angle. Because of the challenges involved in positioning, it is best to start by playing fifths or sixths using the thumb and fifth finger together. This approach provides for a natural position for both fingers.

Five-Finger Exercises and Pieces

(Articulation: Non Legato; Staccato)

Exercise 1

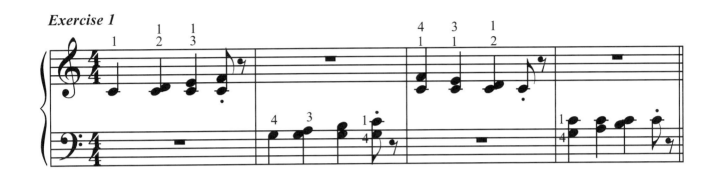

Exercise 2

Exercise 3

Exercise 4

First Steps
Two Easy Pieces for Piano 4 Hands

1

Samuel Maykapar
(1867 – 1938)

43

44

Samuel Maykapar
(1867 – 1938)

46

The Crane

Anton Arensky
(1861 – 1906)

47

Orange Choo-choo Train

Michael Shukh

Study No.1

Ludwig Shitte
(1848 – 1909)

Moderato

49

Study No.2

Ludwig Shitte
(1848 – 1909)

50

Development of Motor Skills*

As mentioned above, developing finger articulation should not be the main goal in the preparatory stage of building the pianistic apparatus. Nevertheless, the finger - the most sensitive and active component of the arm—should not be denied active movement. It is equally essential to take into account that attaining fine motor skills is vital for the harmonious mental and physical development of the child. Relatedly, doing exercises that focus on developing the moving capabilities of the fingers is recommended.

Exercises Away from the Piano

Exercises that focus on swift, "grabbing" finger movements promote a faster reaction time and an awareness of the full arm. They also enhance the strength and efficiency of the muscles responsible for finger movement. For the following, I use a medium-sized silk or chiffon scarf:

1. The teacher tosses the scarf to the student while the student catches it with one hand, using a swift motion from above. The full arm is engaged from the torso.

2. With the palm facing downward, the student holds the scarf in his or her hand, releases the scarf and then catches it again with the same hand, without changing the orientation of the palm (still facing down and wrist unbent).

Finger movement is more natural when the finger is allowed to move in full stride. Following exercises are designed to stimulate the sensation of the finger as an independent, solid tool:

3. **"The Lifting Crane:"** The student can be asked to lift a pencil from a surface, using his or her thumb and third finger. This exercise should also be repeated with the second and fourth fingers, in combination with the thumb. In the moment of the action, the hand should remain soft and relaxed, while the fingers move swiftly and precisely.

4. **"Hide and show:"** The student bends his or her thumbs in such a way that they touch the middle of the palms. The other fingers stretch fully up and then bend to cover the thumb. Repeat a few times.

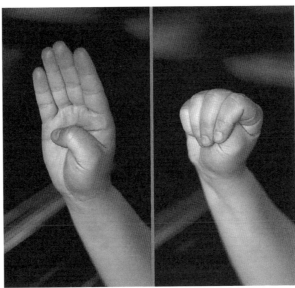

---

*The content from the Development of Motor Skills and Playing Legato chapters should be studied concurrently.

5. **"Running:"** In a sitting position, using finger combinations 2-3 and 3-4, the student "runs" the fingers atop his or her own upper legs.

6. **"Marching Soldiers:"** The student places his or her forearms (up to the elbows) on a table. The palms of the hands are face down. The fingers are placed up on their tips so that the hand assumes a slightly cupped position, the thumb remaining flat on the surface. Each pair of fingers (2-3, 3-4, and 4-5) is then lifted and struck, one after another, in rhythmic fashion. The distal phalanges of the fingers should not be lifted higher than the wrist. It is important that the student rests between repetitions of this exercise, and continuously observes the overall comfort of the hand. The force applied should gradually increase so that the "marching" sound becomes progressively more audible.

When I wish to instill in my students the sense of active finger work, I often ask them to play through passages of pieces on the piano lid or on a table. This is particularly useful for music in which well-developed finger articulation is of utmost importance.

Exercises and Pieces for the Development of Motor Skills
(Articulation: Legato; Staccatto)

A general rule for practicing following piano exercises and pieces is to establish each small movement in slow tempo. When the tempo increases, the individual movements are barely perceptible under the unified movement of the arm. One should aim for a harmonious interaction between active fingers and the rest of the playing apparatus.

It is somewhat dangerous for beginner pianists to play with isolated fingers that are lifted too high as it can cause fatigue in the apparatus, which, in this manner of sound production, is in a state of fixation. However, a lift of the finger should not be completely avoided, as our ultimate goal is to encourage finger liveliness and independence, and avoid excessive wrist movement. As in the exercise "Marching Soldiers," not exceeding the lift of the finger beyond the level of the wrist is recommended. The fingers should remain a part of the pianistic apparatus and interact with the forearm. The use of the forearm, engaged in helpful rotation movements, will prevent any unwelcome vertical movements of the wrist, which typically occur when children attempt to play with isolated fingers.

The forearm rotation movements are especially important in cases where exercises involve the use of the 4th and 5th fingers, which are the weakest and least independent. In these exercises, the forearm helps these fingers create a lift (slightly leaning away from the key) and assists in transferring weight to the fingertip for good quality sound production during key depression. Following the action of pressing the key, there should be a momentary relaxation of the forearm, as no further depression of the key is necessary. The forearm springs back up, as if from a push, which is necessary for returning it to a position that allows for another "grip" of a key. This cycle then repeats.

While in a slow tempo, an exercise may be performed with an emphasis on each note, controlling the lift of the fingers and perceiving a deep sound. The manner of execution changes as the tempo increases. First and foremost, it is essential to view each sequential exercise as a complete structure (motive). In the moderate tempo, the supportive rotation movements of the forearm become less noticeable as the role of horizontal movements increases. The arm guides the hand in the desired direction. The wrist is following the melody line and working in cooperation with the fingers.

The ability to play three to five notes at a quick tempo using one smooth motion of the arm is the first step toward virtuosity. The first note of each motive in exercises 2 through 9 should be played with a feeling of support. To achieve this, it is necessary to bring the arm down from above (this is important for creating momentum, required for establishing a naturally unifying movement of the arm), while the other notes are executed in one "breath", using a light touch of the very sensitive fingertips. The lifting of the fingers decreases, and the movement of the wrist, according to the different melodic contours, becomes less noticeable. The unifying movement finishes on the note, marked with a dot under a slur. This last sound should be executed by releasing the key from the finger's tension and gently pulling the distal phalanx of the finger towards the torso, with the wrist gently moving up (as if swiping a piece of lint off the key with the finger), while completely freeing the hand of any tension.

Finger Staccato

In order to create a short, but ringing sound on the piano, a *staccato* touch is utilized, in which the fingertip vigorously touches the key, almost plucking at it. (To best illustrate the concept of this finger activity, a stringed instrument may be used: If the child is asked to pluck a guitar string, he or she would immediately understand the essence of the kind of approach necessary on the piano for finger *staccato*, imitating this "plucking" action.) The wrist establishes the springing motion. Cooperative movement of the finger and the wrist promote the upward rebound of the finger together with the hand, after which the hand returns back down for the next key. I usually associate this motion with that of a bouncing ball.

The amount of lift in the forearm is controlled by the tempo: The faster the tempo of a *staccato* passage, the smaller the vertical lift and the more important the large horizontal movements of the arm become. Springing motions of the wrist are minimized; wrist follows the fingers.

The use of *finger staccato* is very helpful in correctly approaching the keyboard, the essence of which is the feeling of gripping the key with the fingertip. This physical sensation is not easy to develop, but it is precisely *staccato* playing that allows for the most active "grabbing" of the key by the fingertip, which is then physically remembered by the fingers. Additionally, the *staccato* movement helps the fingers to retain their heightened sensitivity during key contact, regardless of articulation. For this reason, practicing fast *legato* passages using *staccato* articulation, so that the sense of finger vigor may be retained in the original articulation, is often recommended.

All of the following exercises should be first practiced hands separately, and then with hands together.

Exercise 1

Exercise 2

Exercise 3

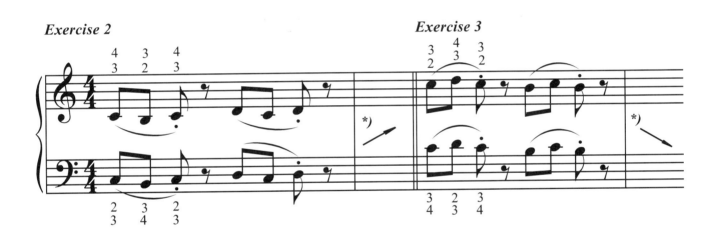

Exercise 4

Exercise 5

*) Continue the sequence

Exercise 6

Exercise 7

Exercise 8

Exercise 9

Exercise 10

*) Continue the sequence

Joke

Vjacheslav Volkov
(1904 – 1980)

Allegretto

Spring Song

Daniel Gottlob Turk
(1750 – 1813)

Vivace

Burlesque

From the Notebook of Leopold Mozart

Buzzing Bee

Michael Shukh

58

Little Dance

Cornelius Gurlitt
(1867 – 1938)

Study

Ludwig Shitte
(1848 – 1909)

Game for Two

Cornelius Gurlitt
(1867 – 1938)

Melody

Cornelius Gurlitt
(1867 – 1938)

Ballett

Daniel Gottlob Turk
(1750 – 1813)

Happy Hours

Daniel Gottlob Turk
(1750 – 1813)

Poco Allegro e scherzando

Coda

Russian Dance

Cezar Cui
(1835 – 1918)

The Cuckoo

Anton Arensky
(1861 – 1906)

Playing Legato

Legato – the ability to play a melody with a singing quality – is the most complex manner of playing on the piano. Only by mastering this type of sound-production will the pianist be able to expand his or her palette of timbral sonorities.

It is best to perceive a type of auditory illusion in which one sound flows into the next. Contrary to the string instruments, the keyboard instrument cannot provide real legato. In order for this illusion to be perceived by the listener, it is vital to make the effect both dynamic and intoned.

Since playing *legato* is perhaps the most wonderful of all goals for an aspiring pianist, it is important to incorporate slow, lyrical pieces into the beginner's repertoire.

Legato Exercises and Pieces

Legato requires a synchronous letting up of one key and depressing of the next. There should be neither an overlap in the depression of the two keys, nor a break in the sound between the two. This entails listening fully until the end of each sound and controlling the changeover to the next.

To articulate proper *legato*, it is best to begin with the use of short, two- and three-note melodic sequences. By connecting two sounds, not only do we learn how to play *legato*, but we also obtain the necessary skills for good phrasing. In piano literature, we continually encounter the resolution of dissonance into consonance; dissonance should be played with an emphatic movement from above, while consonance is imagined as the continued natural extinguishing of the previous sound and is played by releasing the key from the finger's tension and gently pulling the distal phalanx of the finger towards the torso, with the wrist smoothly moving up.

Exercises in which the melodic line contains more than two notes have several aims: The ability to play short phrases in one "breath" with the help of a unifying physical movement, and the capacity to perform this phrase with intoned expressivity through the use of variable dynamics. The weight of the arm, anchored on the fingertip, is distributed according to the required dynamic level. During *crescendo*, the weight of the arm distributed on each finger will gradually increase, while in *diminuendo* it will decrease.

Each of the sequential motivic exercises is to be played at a moderate speed, meticulously controlling the change of one sound to the next. It is as if each finger "hands over" the sound to the next, letting the successive finger gently but deeply depress the next key.

In the performance of longer melodies, it is important to pay attention to the horizontal motion of the arm. The arm guides the hand in the desired direction, much like the bow of a stringed instrument, creating feeling of the long phrase. The wrist movements follow the melody line, though the still active fingers prevent the wrist from excessive motion.

It is important to pay attention to long notes, which are often not held long enough by children. Conversely, unnecessary depression of the key can occur after the sound rings. Once the fingertip physically reaches the bottom of the key, active pressure should cease, though the sense of the finger still holding the key down should be preserved or the sound will fade prematurely. ***One important rule shouldn't be forgotten – the success of legato playing depends on intensive listening.***

69

All of the following exercises should be first practiced hands separately, and then with hands together.

*) Continue the sequence

Exercise 5

Exercise 6

Exercise 7

Exercise 8

*) Continue the sequence

Echo

Andante cantabile

Vjacheslav Volkov
(1904 – 1980)

Lullaby

Andante cantabile

Michael Shukh

Cheerful Hour

Cornelius Gurlitt
(1867 – 1938)

73

Meditation

Vjacheslav Volkov
(1904 – 1980)

Andantino

74

In a Happy Mood

Efrem Podgaits

Allegro moderato

Sad Song

Efrem Podgaits

Snowdrop

Vjacheslav Volkov
(1904 – 1980)

The Lark

Mikhail Glinka
(1804 – 1857)

78

First Steps
Piece in C Major

Samuel Maykapar
(1867 – 1938)

Ten Five-Finger Pieces
Piece in D Minor

Cezar Cui
(1835 – 1918)

83

poco rit.

84

Scales, Chords and Arpeggios

Because scales and exercises are highly patterned and easily remembered, they are much easier to play than *études*. All classical music is woven out of scales and arpeggios. Despite this fact, there is no assurance that being able to play a scale by itself will permit one to play the same scale expressively in a Mozart sonata; it is likely that in the latter context, further challenges will be present. However, being able to command good fingering and to naturally invoke essential movements will undoubtedly influence the speed at which technical problems of any seriousness can be solved. All of the exercises are best learned first with individual hands, as only this will allow for careful control.

Scales

The main musical goal of practicing scales is to achieve evenness of tone at different tempi. In the technical sense, achieving this goal requires well-formed motor skills. The combination of fingers 1-2-3 does not pose a real challenge; problems are likely to appear, however, in the parts of the scale that involve the co-dependent fingers, 3-4-5. It is best to direct the child's attention to this combination, motivating a more active sense of gripping the key with the fingertip (especially with fingers 4 and 5).

An additional challenge in playing scales has to do with uncomfortable shifts in hand positions that involve the thumb (while moving up the keyboard with the right hand or down the keyboard with the left). In order to help the thumb, one should position the hand in such a way as to allow the thumb to be at the desired key ahead of time so that it may be pressed easily and at the correct moment. It is helpful to maintain a feeling that the elbow is leading the forearm in the necessary direction while the wrist turns the hand at the desired angle, allowing the thumb to touch the key ahead of time. This will result in a smooth transition and contribute to the evenness of sound.

In order for the scale to sound more even, it is important to note the particularities of each register; it would be advisable to slightly *crescendo* on the way up, and *diminuendo* on the way back.

Certain techniques for learning scales:

1. Practice in slow and moderate tempo: *Legato*, using active finger movement, while wrist following the melody line divided into tetrachords.

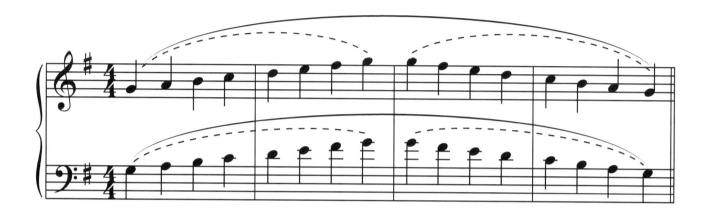

2. Use finger *staccato*.
3. Use dotted rhythm (dotted eighth and sixteenth). The short note should be played using a very active and light movement of the finger, quickly connecting with the following long note, which in turn should be played with weighted emphasis. A stop occurs on the long note. This stop should be long enough to allow student to prepare for the next movement. This method will improve the motion capabilities of each finger.

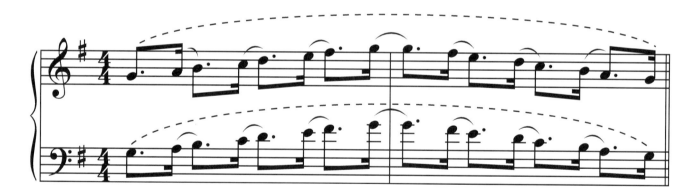

4. In fast scales that are larger than one octave: Perform the scale using active, vigorous fingers but with a light touch and a single arm motion, stopping at first on each fifth note of the scale, and later on each tonic. The stop should be accompanied by a small accent and an immediate release from any tension, while preparing for the next passage.

Playing scales with both hands becomes comfortable when movement synchronization is possible. For this reason, learning to play scales with both hands should first be done using contrary motion, in which the physical movements of the piano apparatus match each other.

Broken Chords

When children play broken triads in continuous inversions, there is typically a gap between the beginning and the end of each group, which breaks the melodic line. In order to connect the sounds, intensive aural attention must be paid to the emerging interval between the fifth and first fingers, while performing a flexible movement of the wrist.

The fingers should be quite active, making sure there are no over-held notes. Each group should be played with an emphasis on the first sound, dropping the weight of the arm. The finger that plays the first note of each group (thumb or fifth) should always be prepared ahead of time. This will help reduce the stretch of the hand and increase the efficiency of movement, which is essential for fast playing. The rest of the group is played with a unifying movement of the arm, ensuring that the elbow leads the fingers while the wrist follows the melodic contour of each segment.

Solid Chords

To prepare for using solid chords, one should first learn to fluently play broken chords as well as blocked intervals. In order to achieve good quality in each sound of a chord, it is essential that the distal phalanx of each finger performs an unnoticeable "grab" at the key. It may be beneficial to use the following exercise: Hold down two notes of a chord, and repeatedly play the third note in *staccato*. Repeat this with each finger. This exercise forces the student's attention to each individual sound of the chord, mobilizing a student to work on a proper touch.

Playing chords with a powerful sound is particularly difficult. Experienced pianists lift their hands as high as possible when playing *forte* chords. For children with small hands, such a lift would necessarily be associated with the risk of hitting the wrong keys. The desired force can be achieved without this risk by having the child rest the fingers on the desired keys and then slightly raise them before pressing down on the keys, using the full arm and its natural weight. This should be accompanied with a movement of the torso in the direction of the keyboard. At the moment the fingers touch the keys, they should feel as though they are pushing the torso away from the keyboard. This should be complemented with a springing movement of the wrists. To avoid a harsh sound, it is important to grab the keys with the tips of the fingers, cushioning a fast drop of the arm.

Much attention should be paid to the fifth finger when playing chord progressions, which tends to be weak and often placed in a flat position on a key.

Arpeggios

Due to the small size of a child's hand, an arpeggio, in preliminary stages of study, should be exercised only in slow and moderate tempo. The following technique should be used: While the right hand moves up the keyboard and the left moves down, it is necessary, as in scales, to maintain a feeling that the elbow is leading the fingers in the right direction. Fingers that finish playing should move together with the wrist, narrowing the stretch of the hand and contributing to greater mobility. This creates a position that allows the thumbs to be prepared for a touch; this positioning also helps the remaining fingers to comfortably move over the thumbs to the next group of the arpeggio. It is important to maintain this narrow hand position by keeping the fingers unstretched when moving with the right hand down and the left hand up the keyboard. Arpeggios should be conceived in short motives, starting with the second note of each group, while the first sound of each group serves as a point of relaxation. Arpeggios are best played with slightly flatter fingers. It is important, however, that they do not lose contact with the keys.

DANCE VOYAGE

Minuet

The name of this dance comes from the French, *pas menu* ("small step"). At one point, the minuet was a circular folk dance in the French province of Poitou. Toward the end of the seventeenth century, the minuet became the most beloved dance of the royal courts. Its character became ceremonious and graceful, exemplified by squats, bows, and curtseys.

Although danced not only within sparkling royal balls, but in more relaxed settings as well, the minuet was considered the preeminent dance of the upper-class ballroom in the eighteenth century. It was referred to as "the king of dances, and the dance of kings."

In the second half of the eighteenth century, the minuet began to be incorporated into various instrumental genres, such as the sonata, symphony, and quartet.

Anonymous
From the Notebook of
Anna Magdalena Bach

90

Minuet

Wolfgang Amadeus Mozart
(1756 – 1791)

Gavotte

Gavotte

The gavotte originated as an ancient folk dance that was performed in lines and circles. Typically very rhythmical and lively, it was accompanied by folk songs and bagpipes.

The gavotte gained its popularity in the French court in the eighteenth century. The movements of dancers became more extravagant. The leading composer of the court, Jean-Baptiste Lully, incorporated the gavotte into ballet and opera, while other prominent composers (such as Bach and Handel) included gavotte in their instrumental suites.

Most often, the gavotte is written in a binary form, where the second part can be presented as a musette – a cheerful pastoral dance, often based upon the characteristic drone bass.

Gavotte

Carl Reinecke
(1824 – 1910)

Musette

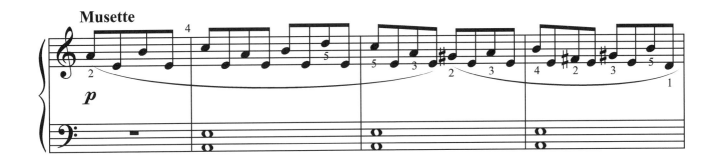

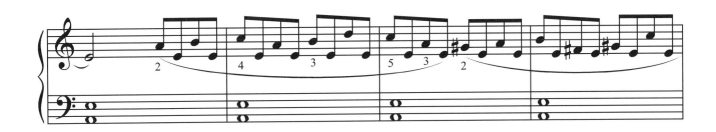

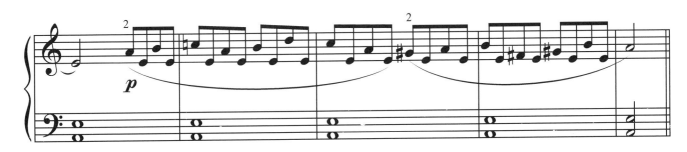

95

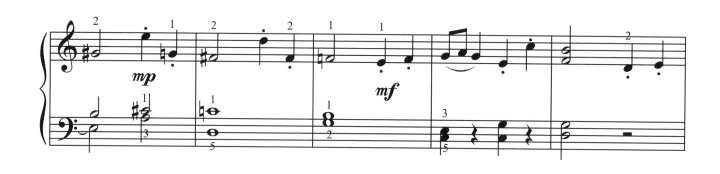

Polonaise

Polonaise

The polonaise is thought to have evolved from the Polish dance melodies that were popular at the end of the sixteenth century. Originally a grand marching dance performed by soldiers, it transformed into a court dance at the opening of a ball and marked the ceremonial quality of the event. The basic step of the polonaise reflects its triple meter, with the stress on the first beat in each measure combined with a longer step that is followed by two shorter steps. Nobility and pride are two main characteristics of the dance.

In the seventeenth century, the polonaise became popular throughout Europe, especially in Germany. Prominent classical composers started to incorporate the polonaise into their instrumental suites.

In the nineteenth century, the minuet lost popularity and was replaced by the polonaise, which became the prelude to the balls of the highest echelons of society.

The polonaise borrowed certain characteristics from the minuet, such as gracefulness and refinement.

The greatest Polish composer of polonaises in the nineteenth century was Frederic Chopin, whose works for piano made this dance the musical symbol of Poland.

Wolfgang Amadeus Mozart
(1756 – 1791)
From "Viennese Sonatina" K439b No.5

99

Mazurka

Mazurka

The mazurka (Polish: *mazurek*, also *mazur*) has its origins in a Polish dance. This dance, called the *mazur*, was very gusty, rhythmically capricious, and used sharp accents on the weak beats of the bar.

In the nineteenth century, the mazurka became a ballroom dance at royal courts, a turn that altered the character of its performance: the stomping and skipping of couples, streaming down the room, was replaced with fluent gliding and circling and far more delicate and noble movements. Despite the changes to the dance, the mazurka's syncopated rhythm, marked by the displacement of the strong beat, remains crucial to this day, as does the dotted rhythm, which was traditionally observed by the stomping of the heels and spurs.

The most popular mazurkas for pianists are written by Frederic Chopin, who employed the characteristics of the mazurka in his own intimate genre. While the polonaise was Chopin's debut in composition, the mazurka remained his last word.

Cornelius Gurlitt
(1820 – 1901)

Mazurka

Samuel Maykapar
(1867 – 1938)

Allegro non troppo

103

Waltz

Waltz

If you have ever seen how a waltz is danced, you will understand why it bears such a name. The word originates from the old German word *Walzer*, which translates to "turning, spinning, and sliding in dance."

As with many other types of dances, the waltz was at one time a folk dance. The ländler, a country dance in 3/4 time that was popular in Bohemia, Austria, and Bavaria, and contributed to the evolution of the waltz, *served to decorate the festivities of peasants. Later, composers such as Mozart, Beethoven, and Schubert created compositions in this traditional old style.*

The dance became especially popular at the end of the eighteenth century in Vienna, a prevalence which led to its becoming known as the Viennese Waltz. It was at this time that its sound changed, becoming more flexible and smooth, gentle and light. Throughout the nineteenth century, the waltz was one of the most popular dances in the ballroom.

Many classical composers wrote in the style of the waltz – the best examples are Chopin, Brahms, Tchaikovsky, and Ravel. The waltzes of these composers are musical performance pieces rather than music for dance.

Lendler
Composition for Piano Four Hands

Franz Schubert
(1797 – 1828)
arr. by F. List

Waltz

Viktor Kosenko
(1896 – 1938)

Tempo di Valse lento

Accompaniment in Dances – Waltz, Polka

Accompaniments in dances traditionally consist of a low bass on the strong beat and a chord or interval on the weak beat(s). Although accompaniments are not less important than melodies, children will usually focus solely on the solo part, neglecting to pay attention to the accompaniment. However, just as a good singer would not be able to sing her best with a poor accompanist, so will our right hand be unable to play the melody expressively without the rhythmic and aurally-balanced support of the left.

The bass should be played with emphasis (the strength depends on the musical idea), using an active finger action that imitates the plucking of a string. The arm shifts with an arched movement from the bass to the chords/intervals in advance, to prepare for the sound production. The chord/interval should sound softer than the bass, and should be played with sensitive fingertips, using minimal arm weight (soft staccato) and springing the hand back to the next bass with the arched movement of the arm. It is best to use different fingering for the bass note and the lowest note of the chord/interval.

It is important to remember that left hand should be carefully practiced alone to maintain proper touch and dynamic balance. If the composition makes use of the pedal, then the left hand should be practiced with the pedal.

In performance, like a good accompanist aware of dynamic articulation and phrasing of the soloist's part, the left hand should follow the melody with care and sensitive support.

Polka

Polka

As in the case of many other dances, the polka has its roots in folk. It is an old, lively Czech dance in duple meter, based on gentle half-steps and turning skips. The polka is danced by couples, usually in a large, clockwise-moving circle.

During the nineteenth century the polka gained popularity as a ballroom dance in Europe. The polka travelled to America with European immigrants and found its place there in theatres and dance halls.

The vibrant spirit of *polka* caused it to be the great inspiration for many classical composers of the nineteenth and twentieth centuries. Smetana, Dvořák, Strauss, Bizet, Tchaikovsky, Rachmaninoff, and Shostakovich left us exceptional instrumental pieces in the style of the polka.

Viktor Kosenko
(1896 – 1938)

110

111

Trio

Da capo al Fine

112

March

March (It. *Marcia*, Fr. *Marche*, from the French word *Marcher* - "to go"): A mostly military musical genre with distinctively crisp rhythms, the march originated as a natural support for the organized movement of the people. Percussion instruments are often used in performance to underscore its rhythm.

In addition to its utilitarian nature, the march has also gained the status of an independent musical genre. Marches are found in the earliest collections of keyboard music. For example, *Anna Magdalena Bach's Notebook* contains three marches. Famous Baroque composer Jean-Baptiste Lully introduced the march into the opera and ballet. In the nineteenth century, the march was heard not only in operas, but also in symphonies. Often, this character piece becomes a movement in a cycle of piano pieces, including those that were composed specifically for children.

Philipp Emanuel Bach
(1714 – 1788)

From the Notebook of
Anna Magdalena Bach

114

Robert Schumann

Album for the Young, op. 68

Robert Schumann (1810-1856) - preeminent German composer of the Romantic period. He was also a conductor, pedagogue, and music critic.

At the age of seven, Schumann began taking piano lessons and improvising. When he was just twelve years old, he composed his first serious composition for a choir and orchestra, based on the 150th biblical psalm. This was a remarkable feat for a child who had no formal instruction in compositional theory. Alongside music, Schumann was passionate about literature and poetry; this ardor is clearly demonstrated in his later compositions in which literary and musical themes became closely intertwined. The boy's artistic talent was clearly evident, but his parents insisted on a more "solid" profession, a frequent occurrence in nonmusical families. Despite his parents' desire, Schumann's university career was short. Throwing aside his studies in jurisprudence, Schumann enthusiastically embraced piano-playing. A later hand trauma would unfortunately prevent him from becoming a virtuoso pianist, but the same event would drive him to focus entirely on composition.

Out of the numerous piano cycles by Schumann (*Carnaval, Papillons, Kreisleriana*), two unique ones, dealing with themes of childhood, can be identified: *Scenes from Childhood* and *Album for the Young*. While *Scenes from Childhood* is a nostalgic reflection on youth, *Album for the Young* is childhood itself, incorporating childhood themes of happiness and sadness, achievement and loss, and the great anticipation of miracles on New Year's Eve. The compositional history of *Album for the Young* is undeniably similar to the compilation a century earlier by the genius composer, J. S. Bach, and his wife, Anna Magdalena Bach. Together, they created a notebook of pieces with the purpose of teaching their own children. Schumann, who idolized Bach, also imagined composing a few pieces as a birthday present for his daughter Maria, who was turning seven. Schumann wrote that the pieces *"grew directly out of my family life...I wrote the first several pieces as a birthday gift for our oldest child, and before I knew it, one followed another."* There were eventually forty-three pieces, divided into two groups: pieces for younger players and pieces for older players.

Not only did Schumann follow in the footsteps of Bach as a pedagogue, but he also infused some of Bach's spirit into his *Album* by incorporating the style of the master in two of the cycle's chorales. Schumann quotes another of his favorite composers in his *Soldiers' March*, using the theme from the Scherzo movement of Beethoven's "Spring" sonata for piano and violin, op. 24.

By the time Schumann crafted *Album*, he was already a seasoned master, and he employed many of his compositional techniques in this piano cycle: a polyphony, a variety of phrasing, multifaceted texture, unexpected melodic and harmonic development, unique rhythmic patterns; and, of course, a multitude of moods, intoned expressivity, and incredible poetry – all distinguishing hallmarks of Schumann's style. Schumann's plan was to create a collection of pieces not only for his own daughter, but also as a teaching tool for other children. He includes guidelines in his book, *Rules for Young Musicians* that are still very useful today.

The first edition of Schumann's *Album for the Young* included vignettes (illustrations/ornamentations) by the German artist, Ludwig Richter. For example, *First Loss* is accompanied by an illustration of a young girl mourning a dead bird, a sad event that took place in the Schumann home. The famous artist's son, Heinrich, wrote in his memoirs that Schumann – under whom he had studied composition – invited Ludwig to his home to listen to the compositions, played by Schumann's talented wife, Clara. During her performance, Schumann provided details about the characters in each of the pieces so that Richter would have more background as he began to illustrate the edition.

Melody

Soldier's March

Lively and precise

Folk Song

As in the beginning

Happy Farmer

Sicilian Dance

Fine

*From the beginning
without repetition
to the word* **Fine**

First Loss

At a moderate tempo

Pyotr Ilyich Tchaikovsky

Children's Album, op. 39

Pyotr Ilyich Tchaikovsky (1840-1893) – the first of the Russian composers whose music made a lasting impression internationally. His well-known ballets, Sleeping Beauty, Swan Lake, and Nutcracker, became classical favorites for many generations of young music lovers. Children's Album is Tchaikovsky's only piano composition written expressly for children.

Tchaikovsky felt the sharp impact of music at a very early age. Although the sounds of the piano rang about the house occasionally, it was not through live performance that the young Tchaikovsky was first awestruck. The impressionable child first discovered the ideal beauty of music through Mozart's Don Giovanni, when he heard Zerlina's aria played on an orchestrion (a machine that plays music and is designed to sound like an orchestra or band). Observing his passion, Tchaikovsky's parents called upon an acquaintance that played the piano to teach the boy, but he quickly outpaced her in his sight-reading ability. At this time, he also began composing. Tchaikovsky's parents found it impossible to provide professional musical education, pushing the young boy to pursue more realistic career. Only at the age of twenty, and after retiring from a boring clerk position, did Tchaikovsky begin his formal music training. He was accepted to the St. Petersburg Conservatory, where he fully answered his life calling.

In the spring of 1878, after travelling through Europe, Tchaikovsky returned to his homeland and stayed as a guest of his sister's in Ukraine. He enjoyed spending his free time with his young nephews, who were studying music. It was then that Tchaikovsky decided to write a set of easy children's pieces. Drawing his inspiration from Schumann's *Album for the Young*, written some thirty years earlier, Tchaikovsky set to his task: "I want to create a full lineup of small selections that are absolutely easy with enticing titles for children, like Schumann." On the title page of the original edition of *Children's Album*, Tchaikovsky mentioned the "likeness to Schumann" and dedicated the work to his nephew, Volodya Davydov.

Children's Album contains several story lines. The cycle opens with a child's awakening (*Morning Prayer, Winter Morning, Mama*). The music progresses to exhibit a day full of children's voices and games: *March of the Wooden Soldiers* and *Playing Horse Games* for boys and a mini-trilogy about dolls for girls. The composer includes in the set some known dances (*Waltz, Mazurka, Polka*), which he had watched at the home of his parents, who had hosted dances at every possible occasion. From his travels around Europe, Tchaikovsky was inspired to include musical sketches based on localized folklore. The influence of Italian folk songs can be observed in *Neapolitan Song*, the theme of which was adapted into *Children's Album* from the ballet *Swan Lake*. Further Italian folk influence can be heard in *Italian Song*. An original French folk melody is heard in *Old French Song*, and a Tyrolean one in *German Song*. Tchaikovsky turns to folk melodies in other pieces as well: *Kamarinskaya* and *Russian Song* are variations on a Russian folk theme. Further, there is a Venetian theme in *The Barrel Organist Sings* and church motives in *At the Church*.

A conventional component of children's albums was the inclusion of specific time periods. For example, Schumann's Album for the Young spans an entire year. By contrast, we encounter Tchaikovsky's heroes for a mere twenty-four hours: The sun sets, evening settles in, and the nanny's storytelling can be heard along with the unmistakable folklore character of an old witch riding her broom (*Baba-Yaga*). The fairy tale comes to an end and the poetic melody, *Sweet Dream*, summons a world of happy dreams. The morning of the following day begins with a lark's song, a prayer, and the repeated motive of the barrel organ, symbolizing the continuity of life.

March of the Wooden Soldiers

Sick Doll

Moderato

Waltz

131

Mazurka

Allegro non troppo
Tempo di Mazurka

134

Italian Song

Moderato assai

Old French Song

Molto moderato

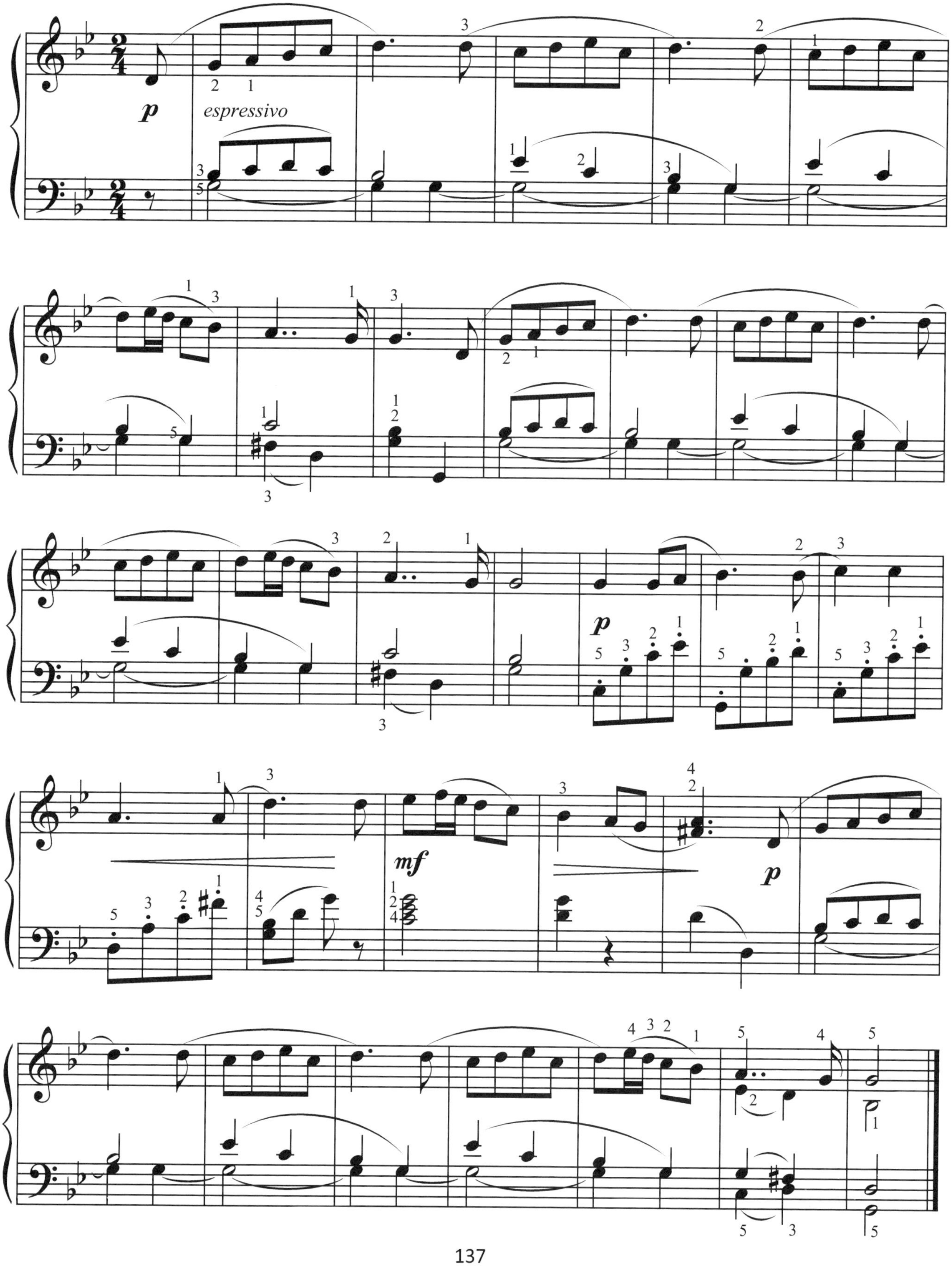

Neapolitan Song

139

Sweet Dream

Samuel Maykapar

Biriulki, op.28

Samuel Maykapar (1867-1938) – famous pianist, composer, and music pedagogue. He authored several books on the art of piano-playing. Maykapar graduated from the St. Petersburg Conservatory as a pianist and composer and completed his studies in Vienna under the famous pianist and professor, Theodor Leschetizky.

Writing music for children is not an easy task. Aside from being a skilled composer, one who wishes to write for children must also be gifted in pedagogy. Maykapar is one of a few composers whose talent was realized through his musical compositions for children.

The name Maykapar is found rather frequently within this book. His best known work is the cycle of piano pieces for children called *Biriulki*. Today, the origins of the word "biriulki" are not well known. The name refers to a once popular children's game, the goal of which was to, using a hook, fish out small pieces from a pile without disturbing the pile as a whole.

In the realm of piano literature for children, the author of *Biriulki* had a predecessor, Anatoly Liadov, who composed a set of fourteen miniatures of his own under the same title. Maykapar's cycle nevertheless retained the greater popularity of the two.

Maykapar's album includes many specific indications relating to articulation, fingering, pedal, and dynamics. In meticulously editing the music, the composer was looking to introduce young musicians to important pianistic and musical techniques that would be useful to them later on. He even devised a special marking to indicate a quickly-executed pedal variation: "*o Ped.*"

Additionally, each piece in the cycle is individual in its character and mode of composition. It is noteworthy that Maykapar, following J. S. Bach, uses all 24 keys in the set and incorporates instrumental and dance genres from the Baroque era (prelude, fughetta, minuet, and gavotte).

Samuel Maykapar's piano cycle has been published in several countries, and in many cases local editors disregarded the composer's precise indications, adding and omitting markings at their own discretion. The current edition, however, offers teachers and their students the unique opportunity to see the music as it was originally published and to perform it the way the composer intended it to sound. This edition is supervised by S. Maykapar's grandson, Alexander, a well-known pianist and performer on historical instruments, and a professor at the Gnessin School of Music in Russia. In this edition, Alexander Maykapar has carefully preserved all of his famous grandfather's notes.

In the Garden

Waltz

Allegretto grazioso ($\jmath$.= 60)

144

Exciting Moment

più agitato e cresc.

poco rit.

a tempo

147

Polka

149

Fleeting Apparition

Little Commander

Allegro marcato ed energico (♩=176)

152

Fairy Tale

Andante dolce e tranquillo ($\half = 76$)

Georgy Sviridov

Children's Album

Georgy Sviridov (1915-1998) – distinguished Russian composer and pianist.

G. Sviridov was born in the small provincial town of Fatezh in southern Russia. The sounds of rustic accordion, balalaika, guitar, and the town bell, as well as melodramatic romances, folk dances, and frequent home singing, were all strong influences in Sviridov's childhood, helping to develop the future composer's musical ear and shape his style.

When the child turned nine, his family moved to the larger town of Kursk, where musical education became a possibility. Sviridov grew proficient in piano and balalaika, and tried his hand at composing – an effort that led to a lifetime of writing music. When he was seventeen, he moved to St. Petersburg (then Leningrad), where he completed his studies under Dmitri Shostakovich. Although Sviridov learned a great amount from his genius teacher, he chose to take a different path compositionally.

Sviridov's individual compositional style was folk-inspired. Dubbing it the "new Russian style," the young composer incorporated his sound into vocal works, ranging from songs to oratorios. Sviridov arrived at this special style after composing his *Children's Album*, which, in his own words, served as a stepping stone toward a new artistic period.

The genre of the children's album was invented by Schumann and was taken up in the nineteenth century by Bizet and Tchaikovsky, and in the twentieth century by Debussy, Grechaninov, Prokofiev and other composers. These masters' inspirations, along with the birth of his son, moved Sviridov to create a cycle of pieces for children. He later wrote his son, Georgy: "I composed an album of little pieces for children – there are now 17 of them. When you were born in 1948, I composed this album for you, so that when you grow a bit you could play these pieces. Now, I have sent the album for publication, so that it may be printed. But it will not be printed very soon – only toward the end of the year. At the top of the score there will be an inscription: 'Dedicated to Georgy Georgievich Sviridov.'"

Sviridov required poetic or visual inspiration in order to compose a new work. His music is both descriptive and poetic. The composer carefully selected the titles for his pieces, ensuring that each of them aided in the characterization of the music. We can easily imagine a girl playing in the bouncing chords of the *Jumping Rope* piece; further, a characteristic motive on a repeated note symbolizes protest in *Stubborn Kid*, and a soft, questioning character is the basis for *Gentle Request*.

The composer taps into his own childhood experiences in the *Album*: the massive sound of the town bell in *The Bells Rang*, which is based on an original Russian folk melody; a young man with an accordion on a village road, performing a joyful dance melody (*Lad with an Accordion*); and an alarmed sense from a frightening Russian fairy tale, in which the main character is an antagonistic sorcerer (*The Wizard*). Furthermore, nature is a very important theme in Sviridov's music. Through an expressive melodic line, the composer portrays the landscape of the coldest Russian season in *Winter*. He depicts the flow of rain drops in *The Rain* using virtuosic trills.

Children's Album is a great tribute, paid to a few idols of the composer's youth. Sviridov includes a march, based on a theme by Mikhail Glinka, the founder of the nationalistic Russian school of composition. The final piece in the cycle is an ode to the style of the German romantics. Sviridov's *Musical Moment* mimics the famous F-minor *Moment Musicaux No.3* by Franz Schubert.

Fairy Lullaby

Jumping Rope

Gentle Request

Stubborn Kid

Allegro non troppo

Musical Moment

161

163

Once Upon a Time There Was a Princess
Fairy-Tale

Theodor Kullak
(1818 – 1882)
Op.62

165

Little Cradle Song

Sunday Morning

169

On the Playground

Alexander Lokshin (1920 – 1987)

Three Pieces for Children

Dance

Waltz

176

Autumn Rain

179

Mikhail Zhuravlev

Inventions

In every age, the primary source of musical ideas for the composition of serious classical music has been folk music. As Mikhail Zhuravlev travelled across Russia, the folk songs and tunes he encountered along the way became the essence of his own inventions. The word "invention" comes to us from J. S. Bach, who used this title for the two-voice polyphonic pieces he composed for his students. The inventions of Mikhail Zhuravlev are also two-voiced, each of them using a particular polyphonic device.

In the **Merry-Go-Round** invention, the composer uses a contrasting polyphonic technique in which the two voices are independent of one another in their rhythmic and intervallic structures. In bars 3-5, the left hand contains a genuine sixteenth-century melody.

In the invention **Swing**, we hear ostinato variations (those that are based on repeated themes in the bass) on a tune from a wedding march notated in a village in Belarus.

Bitonality (the simultaneous use of two different keys) is presented in **Hide and Seek**. One might imagine two musicians simultaneously playing entirely separate pieces while at the same time creating a wonderful duet. This is precisely the magic of polyphony – the individual beauty of each theme, combining harmoniously into a multi-voiced ensemble.

In some instances, the composer did not provide tempo, dynamic, and articulation markings, an intentional choice that would inspire the performer to experiment with the piece in his or her own manner.

Merry-Go-Round

Swing

183

Hide and Seek

SONATINAS/VARIATIONS/BAGATELLE

Sonatina

Part I

Daniel Gottlieb Steibelt
(1765 – 1823)

Alberti Bass

In performing the Alberti bass, it is important not only to keep a steady rhythm and clear articulation, but also to differentiate melodically between any repeated notes and the moving melody line. The repeated note in the Alberti bass is usually played with the thumb. The thumb, in this case, should play lightly, with only minimal vertical movements, practically never leaving the surface of the key. The rest of the fingers play with more emphasis. The direction in which the hand moves is from the thumb to the lower fingers. It is beneficial to play the following exercise: Hold down the repeated note with the thumb, and play the other notes, rotating the forearm with an opening/closing motion of the hand, resembling a flapping wing.

Adagio

188

Sonatina

for Piano Four-Hands

Carl Maria von Weber
(1786 – 1826)
Op.3 No.1

191

192

194

Variations on the Russian Theme

Samuel Maykapar
(1867 – 1938)
Op.8 No.14

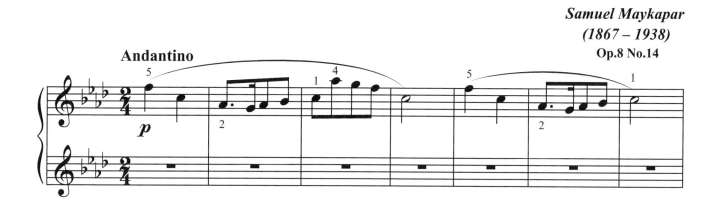

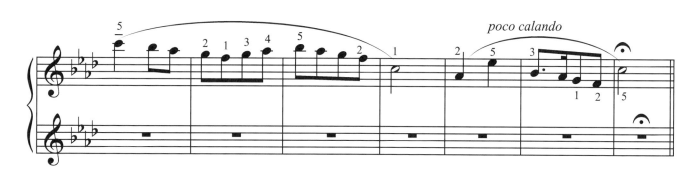

197

CANON
Tempo di Tema

201

Lustig – Traurig

Da Capo al Fine

Waltz for Barbie

Valery Saparov

205

Blues for Barbie

WE PLAY JAZZ

Three Easy Pieces for Piano Four Hands

With a Smile

Valery Saparov

First Waltz

First Waltz

Roly-Poly Doll

Made in the USA
Lexington, KY
10 September 2014